LOVE FROM BEYOND THE GRAVE —CONCLUSIVE PROOF!

Undying Love is packed with documented first-person accounts of life and love from the Other Side. Here is graphic evidence that even skeptics dare not deny!

- FAREWELLS FROM AFAR—As loved ones depart this life, they bid good-bye to those they leave—from thousands of miles away!
- GUARDIAN ANGELS—Those who've left us refuse to let loved ones make life-shattering mistakes!
- A COMFORT FROM THE BEYOND—Those you've loved can stay with you for the rest of your life . . . You need never be alone!
- RELIEF FROM ILLNESS—How the departed help with the afflictions of those who remain!
- OUT-OF-BODY EXPERIENCES—How they confirm the existence of life and love on another plane!
- NEAR-DEATH VISIONS—Not really visions at all . . . A look at the new life to come!
- AND MUCH MUCH MORE!

ALL TRUE CASE HISTORIES!

UNDYING LOVE

BRAD STEIGER
and SHERRY HANSEN STEIGER

BERKLEY BOOKS, NEW YORK

The names and identifying characteristics of persons in this book have been changed to protect their privacy.

UNDYING LOVE

A Berkley Book / published by arrangement with the authors

PRINTING HISTORY
Berkley edition / December 1992

All rights reserved.
Copyright © 1992 by Brad Steiger and Sherry Hansen Steiger.
This book may not be reproduced in whole
or in part, by mimeograph or any other means,
without permission. For information address:
The Berkley Publishing Group,
200 Madison Avenue,
New York, New York 10016.

ISBN: 0-425-13536-5

A BERKLEY BOOK ® TM 757,375
Berkley Books are published by The Berkley Publishing Group,
200 Madison Avenue, New York, New York 10016.
The name "Berkley" and the "B" logo
are trademarks belonging to Berkley Publishing Corporation.

PRINTED IN THE UNITED STATES OF AMERICA

10 9 8 7 6 5 4 3 2 1

CONTENTS

1

The Promise of Undying Love

When you lose someone you love through death, the whole world changes. The flow of life as you once knew it has been severely interrupted. You must face the reality that things will never again be the same as they once were. Whether you have lost a sweetheart, a spouse, a child, a parent, or a dear friend, you will never again see that loving face, hear that gentle voice, embrace the wonder of that person's energy.

But many men and women who have suffered such losses protest against the finality of the grave. They testify that it is not true that our loved ones are lost to us forever. They affirm that the power of love is undying and can conquer even death itself.

There is nothing holier in life than love. True love is a divine gift that cannot be taken away— even by the cold embrace of the Grim Reaper.

India Ingram and Ray Warhol had been sweethearts since their puppy-love days back in elementary school. Ray had forever won India's heart when he stoutly defended her at recess time from the bullies who were picking on the "new girl with the weird name." From that moment of truth when Ray faced down the hulking Bobby Buchinski and his gang of third-grade weasels, India knew in her very soul essence that she would never look at another boy.

Three weeks before the beginning of their junior year in high school, India's parents were transferred to another city. The two teenagers were heartbroken. There was no way that they could endure a separation of several hundred miles. Such a tragedy could not be happening in *their* lives. They weren't star-crossed lovers, like Romeo and Juliet. They had been destined to be married since Mother Eve had started to walk upright. They had talked all summer about the proms, the games, the parties that would enliven their final two years in high school.

At first they had talked of running away and getting married. They were both sixteen, tall and well proportioned, and they looked mature enough to lie about their ages and to be believed by a Justice of the Peace.

But common sense and an eavesdropping younger brother prevailed. They decided to postpone their wedding, and they sat quietly on India's front porch swing carefully pronouncing their preliminary vows.

They promised to write to each other religiously every day. They would visit one another during every holiday. They would plan to attend the same college upon graduation from high school, where they would then be able to continue their romance as more mature young people. They would marry exactly one month after college graduation. India pricked their forefingers, and they each signed their names with a droplet of their own blood smeared on the tip of a ballpoint pen.

One night after the teenagers had been separated for a few months, Ray lay on his bed with his social studies book on his lap. Mom's good cooking and the extra wind sprints at track that afternoon had begun to take their toll on his ability to concentrate. He had just been drifting off to sleep when he was snapped back to full awareness by strange wisps of smoke moving toward him.

Ray's first thoughts were that there must be a fire in the house, but he could not smell anything burning. He knew that he should get up to investigate, but he felt "really weirded out," peculiarly apathetic, almost completely immobile. He was somehow contented to lie still and to watch the mysterious clouds of smoke swirl about in his room.

But within a few moments, the tendrils of smoke had congealed into the shape of a human body. Soon features were discernible, and Ray was openmouthed with shock when he began to recognize an image of his beloved India.

He rubbed at his face with his palms and ground his fists into his eyes. "I could not believe my eyes," he said. "I had to be certain that I was not dreaming. I got off my bed and started toward the cloudy thing that had become India. Before I could touch it, though, it gave me a sad smile and disappeared."

Ray remembered that he was totally dumbfounded. He sat back on his bed, feeling as if all the blood had been drained from his body.

"I felt sick," he said. "I knew that something had happened to India."

Although it was late—nearly eleven—and his parents had strict rules against his running up whopping long-distance telephone bills to India, Ray grabbed his telephone from his desk and quickly punched out the number to the Ingram home.

After four rings, he hung up. Everything must be all right, he told himself. This late at night, India would be prompt to pick up the telephone, certain that it would be his call. He didn't dare let the phone ring any longer for fear of waking India's folks, who were early risers.

As a nine-year-old child, Ray had acquired the habit of keeping a daily journal in which he kept an account of all significant personal experiences. When he had regained his emotional control, he went to his desk and recorded the date and the hour at which he had perceived the image of India.

Two days later, Ray and his parents received word that India and her younger brother had been killed when the car in which they had been riding stalled on the tracks at a railroad crossing as the driver tried to beat the locomotive. The time of India's death corresponded exactly to the time that Ray had recorded the appearance of the apparition of his sweetheart.

"I know that India came to say good-bye to me," Ray said, expressing his deep emotional conviction. "I know that she wouldn't leave without letting me know. I feel that she's now kind of like my guardian angel and that someday we will be together again."

Of all the seen and unseen forces that move men and women, none is more powerful than love. In the course of our exploration into the farthermost reaches of the soul, we have collected hundreds of dramatic case histories of spirit visitations which have all been supercharged by the greatest force in the universe—love. In this present volume, we will share many of these inspirational stories with you.

2

A Special Anniversary Kiss

Charlotte Gilchrist suffered the loss of her husband shortly before their silver wedding anniversary. She remembered how happy Barry had been in the days before his sudden passing.

"First of all," Charlotte said, "he promised me that I would get a very special kiss for putting up with his shennanigans for twenty-five years. Once he got over the big production about that quintessential kiss, he would run down a list of extravagant gifts that he claimed he was going to buy for me. Well, he changed the list of presents so often that all I was really certain of getting was that truly remarkable anniversary kiss."

Just a month before their anniversary celebration, Charlotte Gilchrist received a call from a furniture store which presented her with the shocking and sorrowful information that her husband had just dropped dead of a heart attack while purchasing a new sofa.

The anniversary celebration had been transformed into a day of mourning. Charlotte's and Barry's married children and many friends came to visit her and console her; but when they all left that evening, she was alone with an empty house and the gift that she had purchased for her husband.

Slowly she prepared for bed, dawdling over her coldcream application. When she finally turned out her bed lamp, she was astonished to see what appeared to be a pinkish disk approaching her. It continued to grow as it neared her bedside until she could see that the disk had been transformed into the head of her deceased husband.

"Barry's features hovered about four inches away from my face," Charlotte said. "His head kind of wavered, like it was trying to come into better focus; then it was very still.

"There was a kind of illumination coming from his face, and I could look deeply into his eyes. Then he kissed me—a lingering, special kiss.

"I began to cry, but he gave me a wink and that whimsical smile that I knew so well.

"Then, as suddenly as he had appeared, he began to fade away from my sight. Smaller and smaller he became—until there was nothing but that pinkish disk again. And then there was nothing at all.

"Barry had kept his promise. I had received my special anniversary kiss. He had kept his word, even though he had to return from the dead to give it to me."

Images of deceased loved ones who have come to bid fond farewell or to bring messages to those whom they have left behind offer dramatic evidence of the soul's continued existence. Although skeptics may attempt to explain away the manifestation of Charlotte Gilchrist's husband as an hallucination caused by her loneliness and sorrow, she will always cherish the phantom kiss as her personal proof of survival.

"I know that was my Barry and I know that that was his kiss," she stated firmly. "His special anniversary kiss proved to me that we will always be together."

3

Death Could Not Stop Delivery of the Birthday Cakes

Ute Drinkwater from Tulsa, Oklahoma, told how, on her husband's last birthday before he passed away, he had received two elaborately decorated cakes—one from the family, the other from an organization in which the Drinkwaters were active. Sam Drinkwater had retained a child-like enthusiasm for birthdays and holidays, and he had been enormously pleased by the special attention that he had received.

Ute's birthday fell soon after Christmas, and because she had come from a large family who had subsisted on a meager income, she had become accustomed to having her natal anniversary passed over without special notice. The situation had been remedied after her marriage to

Sam, of course, but she still teased him about his receiving two extravagantly large birthday cakes when she had gone so many years without having been given any cakes at all.

"Well, dang it, Mother," Sam laughed. "This year I'll see to it that you receive two big special cakes on your birthday, too. Then we'll be even!"

Sam Drinkwater died one week later from a sudden heart attack, and it would have appeared that he had been freed from all earthly promises and commitments. Such, according to Ute, was not at all the case.

On her birthday, several weeks later, Ute Drinkwater sat quite alone, feeling very sad and depressed. None of her family lived near, and none of her friends knew the date of her birthday. Since it was two days after Christmas, she had chosen not to bother anyone about an additional celebration during the holidays.

With Sam in his grave for nearly two months, there seemed nothing for her to do but to spend a night in solitary misery.

But amazingly, on that cold and icy night, a friend, Lorna Mellenbacker, traveled across the city by bus to deliver a cake and a carton of ice cream to Ute so that they might celebrate her birthday.

"How did you know?" Ute risked rudeness to ask.

"I don't know if you'll believe this or not," Lorna wondered, a nervous smile on her lips. "I had just got home from work when I heard old Sam talking to me as if he were standing right there in the room with me. He told me that it was your birthday and that I should hurry out and buy you a cake!"

Ute was stunned by her friend's explanation of the birthday treat, but she didn't feel like interrogating her any further.

Ute and Lorna had no sooner finished the cake and ice cream when Anita Mendez, the young girl who had been boarding with Ute since Sam's death, entered the front door carrying a box which contained a beautifully decorated birthday cake.

"Anita," Ute shook her head in astonishment. "How did you know it was my birthday?"

Anita could only smile and shrug her shoulders. "I . . . I just felt like buying it for you when I was walking past the bakery."

Ute knew that she had not mentioned the fact that it was her birthday to Anita, and the young boarder had never known Sam.

"My husband kept his promise," Ute Drinkwater said. "He saw to it that I received two special cakes for my birthday."

4

Tony Came for a Final Communion

Adrian Cozza attended Communion the day after her husband had been laid to rest. "I went to the early service that Sunday," she said, "and my thoughts were filled with anguish as I contemplated the long years ahead without my husband, Tony."

Adrian remembered that she sensed a presence next to her in the pew, kneeling beside her. "I knew that it was Tony, but I did not turn to look. I did not want to do anything to destroy the impression I had of his presence. I wanted to hold on to the feeling that Tony had actually returned to take Communion with me."

When Adrian went forward to receive the sacrament at the altar rail, she felt that the presence of her husband walked with her.

"But after I knelt to receive the wafer, I sensed that Tony had once again left me. I was sad, but I was also heartened to have felt him near me so strongly."

A few days later, when she was visiting with her priest, Father Castilla, he told her that he had had a most unusual experience at the early Communion service that Sunday: "As I was turning to face the altar, I had the most peculiar feeling that Tony had come in and had knelt down beside you. When you walked to the altar to receive the sacrament, I had to blink my eyes. It almost seemed as if I could behold a dim outline of Tony standing just behind you."

As Adrian concluded her account: "I received spiritual comfort beyond words to be able to believe that Tony's spirit joined me in church on that Sunday morning to partake of a farewell Communion service with me."

The doubts of the cynical have no relevancy to those who have witnessed the apparition of a dear spouse or a loved one. The scientifically minded may be sympathetic toward the human need to retain physical contact with the beloved deceased, but they are likely to speculate whether the bereaved were truly visited by the actual spirit personalities of their loved ones or whether they were only externalizing their grief.

5

*Unknown Insurance Policies
Materialize for a Wife
in Great Financial Distress*

As serious researchers of spiritual phenomena,
we recognize that the more we discover about the
limitless powers of the human mind, the more
difficult it becomes to establish truly objective,
evidential proof of the interaction of a discarnate
personality in the life of someone who is on the
material plane. However, we have received dozens
of accounts that we feel are far more than the dramatic devices of sorrowing imaginations. In hundreds of cases, the apparitions gave their loved
ones information that was previously unknown to
the bereaved and which could later be verified. In
some instances, this information was provided by
a person known as a spirit medium or channel, a

third party unknown to either the deceased or to the mourning survivor.

Some years ago, the highly respected Chicago medium Deon Frey related the account of a woman who had come to her for psychic counsel because she was in great distress and in need of money. The woman's husband had passed on suddenly, and since he had no insurance policies and a number of debts, he had left his wife and four children virtually penniless. It was a cold fall, and the winter would be even colder. The children needed new heavy clothing, and she needed some money until she could find suitable employment.

"I met her for lunch," Deon said, "and although I was not in trance and we were in a crowded restaurant, I could see distinctly an image of the woman's husband building up behind her. I described the man, and the woman verified that I must be seeing her husband. She began to cry, but I paid little attention to her. The man who was in spirit was telling me something very important.

"He said to tell his wife that he loved her and that he would cherish the memory of her and the children forever. He also said that he had not left her destitute. If she would go down into their basement and look behind the cabinet of old fruit jars there, she would find several loose bricks. If she were to pry them out, she would find three paid-up insurance policies in a tin box. There would be more than enough money there to provide for the children's education and to keep the family functioning comfortably until she was able to find an adequate job."

The woman was shocked and very skeptical.

She knew of no such hiding place, and she knew of no insurance policies. And if such policies did exist, why hadn't she been contacted by agents from the insurance companies?

"I've never gone to a medium before," the woman told Deon. "I mean . . . I don't know about all of this."

Deon could see that the woman was wondering if she was some kook who was just making up a story to tell her. But then the man in spirit spoke to her again.

"Your husband says that he was wrong to have kept the papers a secret," Deon relayed the entity's message. "But he had been paying the premiums on them for many years and he regarded them as a nest egg for his old age and as a comfortable sum for you and the children if he should die. He knows now that he was wrong not to have told you about the insurance policies, but he died so suddenly that he had no time to give you this information. No agents have called on you, because he first acquired these policies when he was a young man out of college back in Milwaukee. The companies have not been notified of his death."

When the woman left Deon, she was shaken, pale, and not entirely convinced. But that night the medium received a telephone call from the woman stating that Deon must truly have made contact with the spirit of her husband. She had looked behind the cabinet of old fruit jars, found the loose bricks, and discovered the insurance policies in a tin box. True to her husband's promise, it appeared as though she and the children would be comfortably situated.

While one must avoid the materialistic machinations of alleged psychic sensitives who deliberately and cruelly prey upon the bereaved who seek communication with loved ones on the Other Side, there seem to be those spiritually blessed men and women who have been given the gift of channeling information from the unseen world.

Once again, the skeptic and the objective researcher may ask if the spirit of the woman's husband had actually spoken through Deon—or if the medium exercised a psychic capacity of clairvoyance to discover the secret of the hidden insurance policies. Telepathy, unless the psychic impulses were transmitted from a discarnate entity, must be ruled out in this case, for no living person knew of the location of the documents.

Deon firmly reiterated the facts of the spirit communication: "First of all I had never met this woman before in my life, and I knew nothing about her except that a mutual friend had asked me to talk to her. Second, I had never known her husband or had any idea what he looked like on the earth plane. Third, I provided the woman with information which no living person knew—information which only the dead man could have provided. Good lord, is this proof of survival or isn't it?"

6

Love Wrapped Up in a Million Stars

Gilbert Infante does not question his proof of life beyond death. He reveres the memory of the experience that demonstrated to him the power of love to pierce the seeming finality of the grave.

Gilbert had left the bedside of his wife, Irene, who was dying of leukemia. The ordeal had been a long and painful one for his poor wife, as well as having been an expensive and exhausting one for him.

"But I will never count the cost," he had told his friends at work. "If I had to be in debt for the rest of my life and could keep my Irene with me, I would never complain for one second."

The insurance coverage had been depleted long ago, and there would be medical debts. Sadly, it now appeared that there would not be his Irene.

They had married within days of his return from Vietnam. They had both had such high hopes for the future. Then, almost right after the birth of Antonia, their second daughter, the doctors diagnosed Irene as having leukemia.

"Please, my love, please go home and get some rest," Irene whispered.

It pained Gilbert's heart to see her so thin, so weak, her beautiful olive complexion so colorless.

"You must not stay here another night worrying about me," she said. "Go home and see to the children."

Gilbert sighed and told her that he would go home for a little while. But only to see if he could assist her mother who had come to help with baby-sitting and the housework. "When I know that Mama is okay with the girls, I will come back to the hospital to be at your side, my angel. Okay?"

Irene only smiled.

Gilbert saw that the girls, Antonia and Elizabeth, were sleeping and that Irene's mother had already gone to bed. He checked his watch, decided that he would nap for just a few minutes before he returned to the hospital.

He could not have been sleeping more than twenty minutes when he felt what he knew to be the touch of Irene's lips on his cheek. "It was a kiss of sweetness and love, a kiss that only Irene could have given me. No one will ever be able to convince me that it was not my wife who kissed me at that moment."

Gilbert opened his eyes and sat up. He had left a small lamp on in the room before he had lain down to rest.

"I knew that someone else was in that room with me," he stated. "Then, in a darkened corner, I caught a movement out of the corner of my eye. I turned to see a figure that seemed to be made up of a million, tiny, sparkling stars. Although I could distinguish no features, the figure had a human-like shape. It seemed to raise its arms and to float up out of sight through the ceiling.

"When I called the hospital a few moments later, I was already prepared to hear that Irene had just died. The night nurse was just about to call me. She spoke a few words to console me, but I had just received the greatest kind of consolation from my Irene, who had come to prove to me that there is life beyond physical death and that love is the greatest power in the universe."

7

A Love Story Beyond the Now

John Harricharan, the award-winning author of *When You Can Walk on Water, Take the Boat* (Berkley, 1990) and the recent *Morning Has Been All Night Coming* (Berkley, 1991) shared with us the following beautiful account of his continuing contact with his wife Mardai, who made her transition a few years ago.

"There are certain scenes and circumstances in life that seem to have been arranged by others with much more intelligence than I could ever credit myself," John said. "One such situation was my marriage to the princess of my dreams. From the first day that I saw her, I knew that there was a bond between us that spanned time, distance, social position, and all earthly obstacles."

John and Mardai had met each other many

years prior to their marriage when they were youngsters in a foreign country. "Though we were later to be separated by great oceans and countries," he continued, "we finally met again and were married. At the time of our marriage, she was only nineteen, and the joy of my life. Together we built a beautiful partnership and met the ups and downs of life. With her by my side and with her constant encouragement, I was able to build a semblance of financial security. After the children came, we were even happier and looked forward even more to the future."

But sadly, as John phrased it, "the cold winds of misfortune" began to blow across their lives. Slowly at first, and then with ever-increasing speed, John lost his business and all of their financial security. It was as if the winter of his life had begun. Mardai, whose very name means "light," became the source of illumination that guided him through the darkness that followed.

"We lost our home and land and most of our material possessions," John stated. "With our two children we finally moved to a new city and started to rebuild our lives from ground zero. I thought that we had suffered enough, but our financial losses were nothing compared to the diagnosis that we received a few months later that informed us that Mardai had cancer. It took a while to get used to such disasterous news, especially since all of us had been relatively healthy and no one expected any problems."

Mardai's battle with cancer was a long and terrible one. Although she fought bravely, she could not prevail, and John lost the light of his life one summer's day. "We had been married for twenty years, and I had no idea how I would continue in life without Mardai. As I stood there that July day holding my two children close to me, the emptiness within me was so horrible that all I could think was, 'Is there no balm in Gilead?' "

In the days that followed, John's thoughts would run races between the sublime and the ridiculous. There were times when he looked around him and perceived life as a meaningless mess. But there were other times when a quiet voice would whisper in his heart that life was not as it appeared to be. Life was much more than a short span on Earth. A lifetime was but a blink in eternity. Slowly, ever so slowly, he began to understand.

Sometimes while driving, he would look at the empty seat next to him—the seat in which she used to sit—and he would wonder where she had gone. "Everyone knows where the caterpillar goes—it goes into the butterfly. But who knows where the butterfly goes?

"So I thought of Mardai as a butterfly of the universe," John stated, "and I would pray that her journey be a joyous one and that she would find some way of letting me know that she was fine in her new world.

"One day as I was thinking such thoughts, I pulled up at a red traffic light behind another car. As I waited for the light to change, I silently said, 'Mardai, if you are around, please let me know. I would feel much better.' The light changed, and as the car in front of me pulled away, I saw on the license plate MEH 711. 'MEH' were Mardai's initials, and '711' stood for July 11, the date she died. A calmness and joy welled up within me, and I heard a voice in my mind say, 'I am with you.' "

John told us that from that experience many others were to follow. "They seemed to come at times when I most needed reassurance about life and its direction. After a while it became commonplace to see Mardai's initials on billboards and license plates, and I would look at a clock for no apparent reason only to find that the time would be 7:11. I became so used to seeing such signs that as time went on, I ignored many of them for fear of becoming too dependent on them. Yet, I found a strange, beautiful comfort in such reminders."

Sometimes John would be thinking of Mardai, and at that very moment a song that she loved would play on the radio.

"It was as if she were saying, 'I just want you to know that I love you and am with you whenever you think of me.'

"It is my belief that our loved ones continue their lives in an area just beyond our physical senses," John said. "I feel that they reach out to help, to guide, to comfort us in a most loving way. There are signs of their presence all around us if we but look more closely and listen more attentively."

Furthermore, John explained, he believes that the bonds that exist between those who love deeply are stronger than death itself. Perhaps, he commented, love is the greatest reality in the universe.

"Although I no longer see Mardai's physical form

nor hear her lovely musical voice, I know that she exists, and I have a notion that she is closer than I think," he said. "Sometimes I meet her in my dreams, and at other times I feel as if she speaks to me in the quietness between my thoughts."

John's father died a few years before Mardai, and he continues to feel his presence as well. "Those whom we love will always be with us," he said.

"Sometimes on a beautiful, cloudless, starry night, I sit on my porch and look into the woods behind my house. I hear the voices of my loved ones in my heart and in the very whispering of the wind through the leaves. I look up into the sky and see the second star on the belt of Orion the Hunter, and I can see Mardai smiling at me.

"As I look and listen in the quietness of my soul, I hear her say, 'I have always loved you, and you will always be my joy, my pride, and my prince. I have known you from eternity, and I will be with you again one day, even as we used to be together in the life you now live.

" 'When you are sad, I feel your sorrow, and when you are happy, I rejoice with you. You must finish the work that you came to Earth to do. Time will lighten the heaviness in your heart, and then I will be able to communicate with you more clearly.

" 'I watch over you and our children, and I know how difficult it can get at times. But you are not alone. There are others here who also watch and help. Our work on Earth was finished, so we had to go on. We are all brilliantly alive.

" 'I visit you sometimes in your dreams. The veil

that separates your reality from mine is very thin indeed. In your quiet moments, you sometimes pierce that veil and obtain a glimpse of our reality. It is gloriously exciting where we are, and one day we shall all meet again. You have much to do before you join us, but know that we will be with you every step of the way.

" 'My dearest John, I have always loved you, and I will love you through the Halls of Forever. When you are ready to come here, I will be the first one waiting to greet you. Live life joyously and fully.' "

John told us that he does strive to live life as gloriously and as fully as he can. His son and daughter are happy, and he has rebuilt a good part of himself.

"I find joy and comfort in the simple things around me," he said. "I know that our loved ones are always with us. I know that love prevails over everything, even over death.

"Listen to your heart, and you will hear the sounds of eternity. You will feel the ties that bind you in an everlasting love. May your journey home be a joyous one."

8

A Former Lover Became Her Guardian Angel

Kevin Lawsky and Doreen Malpeci had known each other for several years and had become good friends long before they had begun to think of each other as potential sweethearts and mates. Their sudden awareness of each other as lovers had one day seemed a most natural thing, and they could not help chiding themselves after having worked in the same insurance company for nearly three years.

Kevin, who Doreen soon learned had a mystical side to his nature, would philosophize that a Force-Greater-Than-They had for some reason seen fit to keep them apart, yet together, for so long. Doreen would sometimes blush when Kevin teased her about the past occasions when she had taken her love-life problems to trusty Kevin, who, at that time, had seemed like an older brother in whom she could confide.

"Perhaps it's true," Kevin said one night as they relaxed with wine and cheese in front of the fireplace in his apartment. "Maybe I was your brother in another lifetime."

"You mean, like in reincarnation?" Doreen had giggled, not completely certain if Kevin were serious or not.

"Sure," he confirmed her assumption. "When do you think we might have been together as brother and sister? I'm kind of picking up a romantic period, like maybe Renaissance Italy. I think I was a painter, and I created a portrait of you in an elegant, flowing gown. It caused a sensation because you were so beautiful and I was so talented. The portrait made me famous overnight."

Doreen laughed at him over the rim of her wine glass. "You are a little weird, you know that, don't you?"

Kevin shrugged. "Well, it could have been. I only know that the moment I saw you I felt very protective toward you. It was as if I wanted to be your bodyguard."

Doreen snuggled up next to him. "You can guard my body forever," she murmured in his ear.

When Kevin proposed marriage, Doreen did not hesitate to give an overwhelmingly positive answer. Kevin was twenty-eight; she was twenty-five. They were old enough to know what they were doing, young enough to enjoy doing it. They had not fallen in love; they had grown in love. Theirs was the kind of ideal relationship that she had read about in the magazines in the beauty shop.

They had been friends before they had become lovers.

Two months before the wedding, Kevin was killed instantly in an automobile accident.

Doreen has little memory of the first few weeks after Kevin's death. "I was left to try to put back together the scattered pieces of what seemed to be an irrevocably shattered life. It was well over a year before I began dating again. I know that I was too hard on the men who asked me out, because, in my mind, no one could ever begin to compare to Kevin. No one could ever satisfy me on as many levels as Kevin had. There were men with whom I didn't mind being friends, but I was not ready to visualize any of them as my lover."

Two years after Kevin's fatal accident, Doreen began to go somewhat steadily with Charles Mybeck. "After three months, he asked me to marry him. I was unable to give him an answer at the time, and I asked for a few days to consider his proposal. I had tender feelings for Charles, but I also felt that I was not ready to marry him just then."

Doreen explained her feelings to Mybeck, but the man continued to court her for nearly a year. Finally Doreen agreed to marry her persistent suitor. On a physical attractiveness scale, Charles was probably better looking than Kevin; but in spite of his impeccable manners, he did not have the depth of feeling that her deceased fiance had revealed. On the purely materialistic side of things, Charles drove a Mercedes and always seemed to have plenty of money.

One night, less than a week before the wedding, Doreen remembered that she had lain tossing and turning in bed, unable to sleep. Her mind was full of thoughts of Kevin, her dead fiance, rather than Charles, her living husband-to-be. Her entire being seemed to be suffused with a strange uneasiness.

"How I wished that it were somehow possible for Kevin to be there to discuss the whole business with me," Doreen said. "I knew that he would be able to give me good advice, just as he had so many times in the past."

She began to cry, and in between her sobbings, she became aware of Kevin's voice calling her name. "I sat bolt upright in bed, struck with the sudden realization that I was not imagining the sound of his voice. I was actually hearing Kevin calling to me!"

Doreen looked in the direction from which the voice seemed to be emanating, and she was startled to see Kevin standing solid as life next to her dresser. So many images began to flood her brain that she feared that she would succumb to the shock of seeing Kevin standing there and faint dead away. Then she became strangely calm and pacified at the sound of his voice.

"Your marriage to Charles Mybeck is a serious mistake," Kevin told her. "You must not marry him. He is not the man for you. He is not what he appears to be."

Doreen was so moved, so impressed by the apparition of her dead fiance that she feigned illness and told Charles that they must postpone their marriage in order to give her time to recuperate.

Two weeks later, Charles Mybeck was arrested on charges of illegally possessing marijuana and such hard drugs as heroin and cocaine. During his hearing, conclusive evidence was produced to prove that Charles was more than a user and a chemical substance abuser, he was a "pusher," a recognized dealer in the illegal drug network. Under examination by the prosecution, it was also revealed that Mybeck was already married and had a wife in an asylum in another state. Tragically, she had become a drug addict under the ministrations of Charles Mybeck, and she had suffered severe brain damage when he had once injected her with some "bad stuff."

Two years later, just a few days before she turned thirty, Joel Raney asked Doreen to marry him.

"I felt almost certain that an apparition of Kevin Lawsky, my dear friend and lover, would once again appear to let me know if my choice was a wise one," Doreen said.

"Three nights before my August wedding to Joel, Kevin appeared in my room. He looked just as solid as he had when he had materialized two years before to warn me about Charles Mybeck. I was not shocked this time, and I waited eagerly for some sign, some signal from him. This time Kevin only smiled at me, waved a hand, and disappeared. I knew that dear Kevin had given my marriage to Joel his blessing and that he had waved his hand in farewell."

One of the great questions most frequently asked about such dramatic tales of undying love is whether or not a lover who has passed over maintains his or her love for the surviving partner. And what if the survivor of the marriage or love affair finds another earthly lover? Does the deceased lover become jealous—or does he or she now exist beyond petty concerns of the flesh?

It would seem, based on such accounts as the one just related about Kevin Lawsky and Doreen Malpeci, that the deceased lover maintains an affectionate interest in the one dearest to him or her who remains on the earth plane. It may be that those reports which tell of discarnate personalities who remain jealous and possessive of their surviving partners are actually accounts of entities which are held unnaturally to the earth plane by obsessive interests which have prevented their translation to higher spiritual dimensions.

9

Comfort From Beyond:
You Are Never Alone!

John Frederik Oberlin, the famous pastor, educator, and philanthropist, literally transformed the whole life of the Ban-de-la-Roche Valley in the Vosges Mountains of Alsace. Shortly after the clergyman's arrival in the district, he expressed his displeasure concerning certain practices of the villagers that he considered distasteful and superstitious. Pastor Oberlin had become especially agitated over the stories that he had heard of the apparitions of loved ones who had passed over. He resolved to educate the simple folk, and he launched a vociferous pulpit campaign against such primitive beliefs.

In spite of his orthodox denial of apparitions, the reports of such spiritual visitations continued

unabated, and Pastor Oberlin was honest enough
to admit that he was beginning to feel his dogma
crumbling around him.

In 1806, a dreadful avalanche at Rossberg buried several villages, and the accounts of visions of
the dying and the dead appearing to their loved
ones became so numerous that Pastor Oberlin at
last came to believe that the villagers were indeed
perceiving spirits of their dear departed.

In *Footfalls on the Boundary of Another World*,
Robert Dale Owen tells us that Oberlin came to
believe that his own wife appeared to him after her
death. The clergyman stated that his wife's spirit
watched over him as though she were a guardian
angel. Furthermore, Pastor Oberlin claimed that
he could see his wife's spirit, talk with her, and
make use of her ethereal counsel regarding future
events.

When a skeptic asked the pastor how he was
certain that he could distinguish his wife's spirit communications from the fantasy of dreams,
Oberlin replied: "How do you distinguish one color
from another?"

John Murietta returned from the Korean conflict an emotionally scarred and embittered man.

While he had been overseas, his wife Angela
had entered the hospital to have a lung removed
because of a malignant tumor. John's twenty-
year-old kid sister, Cyndi, had been minding
his three-year-old daughter Amy, and the two of
them had been killed in an automobile accident as
Cyndi was driving to the hospital so that the child
might visit her mother. When Angela learned of

the deaths of Amy and Cyndi through the careless lips of an indiscreet nurse, the shock proved to be too much for her, and she seemed to lose the will to live. She died four days after her surgery.

Since John's parents had died when he and Cyndi were very young, the soldier came home to an empty house. He had lost his entire family while he was in combat. He had weathered some of the bloodiest campaigns of the Korean war, and his body had returned to the States without a scratch. It was his spirit that had been mangled and bruised.

Murietta received his discharge papers. He toyed with the idea of re-enlisting, then considered the call of an African nation advertising heavily in the European newspapers for mercenaries.

Kyle and Alex, a couple of men he had known in the army, approached him with the idea of leaving for Africa, and they tried hard to sell him on their plan of joining the highly paid professionals who fought for hire. Kyle and Alex were rough, violent men, who loved war and killing. He had never associated with them while they served together in Korea, but now that he was all alone, John reasoned, why not grab the money and run. His rifle could kill as well as the next man's.

Only one factor caused Murietta to hesitate to give his decision to Alex and Kyle. Before he had shipped out to Korea, he and Frank Avila, Cyndi's fiance, had talked about opening a custom garage together. John knew that Frank had been drafted shortly after he himself had been sent to Korea, but he had had no news from him since Cyndi's death.

Although he and Frank would one day have been brothers-in-law—and they had become friends upon their first meeting—John did not know Frank's parents' full name and address. Maybe, he thought desperately, if he could somehow contact Frank and find out when he was getting out of the army, he would forget about Africa and just get a temporary job in their hometown until Frank was discharged.

On the other hand, shooting a rifle in Africa for a few months could bring a lot of money fast—enough money to put a down payment on a garage.

One Sunday morning, John was sleeping late. He rolled over to see what time it was, then opened his eyes wide when he saw the solid image of Angela, his wife, standing at his bedside.

"She gave me her brightest smile," he said. "She was just as pretty as I would always remember her."

John will never forget the message that Angela relayed. "Try to have the courage to get through these bad days," she told him. "I am happy here. So are Cyndi and Amy. Oh, and Frank is here with us, too. He and Cyndi came over together. We are concerned about your companions. We don't want you to go to Africa. We don't want you to kill anymore. We love you and we will always be with you. You are not really alone."

Before John could move or speak, the vision of his wife had disappeared from his sight. "I had so much wanted to hold her, to touch her, to talk to her; but it was like she just evaporated."

As the day wore on, however, John became more skeptical about the apparition. He had always prided himself on being a hard-nosed pragmatist who had never believed in anything that he could not hold in his hands and see with his own eyes. Perhaps, he reasoned, he had been too preoccupied with thoughts of his family's death and the question of whether or not he should join Kyle and Alex on their mercenary trek to Africa.

The apparition of Angela had given him one bit of information which would prove to be disheartening if true, but which could be checked out if he could somehow contact Frank Avila's parents. According to the spirit of Angela, Frank was also dead and had died on the same day that Cyndi had been killed.

At last John thought of Estelle Johnson, a girl friend of Cyndi's, who worked in a neighborhood bank. Perhaps she could tell him more about Avila. Estelle and Cyndi had been very close.

To John's great relief, Estelle did know the names of Frank's parents and the suburb in which they lived. He called them that night and he learned that Frank had been killed in action in Korea on the very day that Cyndi and Amy had been killed in the automobile accident.

Angela's spirit had told him the truth, and even though John Murietta should have felt even more alone than ever after learning of the death of Frank Avila, he turned down the proposition of his mercenary friends and decided to get a job that would enable him to rebuild his life in a positive way.

* * *

"I'll always remember the words that Angela spoke to me from that vision," John said. " 'We love you and we will always be with you. You aren't really alone.' "

10

Piano Practice in Heaven

When Owen Martin was a young boy, his family lived in a small village near Spring Green, Wisconsin. In late January of 1928, the granddaddy of all blizzards seized the area and drifted white mountains of snow across the fields and the highways. Owen remembered that this blizzard was particularly vicious because of the sharp, icy winds that it brought with it, winds that seemed to penetrate the heaviest wool coats and the thickest storm windows.

In those days, families provided most of their own entertainment, and the Martin family was blessed with their little Denise, a virtual child prodigy at the piano. At the age of seven, Owen stated, his little sister was already a popular featured soloist at church socials and Sunday band concerts in the park.

"Every night Denise would practice, perfecting her craft, improving her talent," Owen said. "We would read books and magazines when we had finished our homework and sometimes we would listen to some news or comedy on the radio, but Denise provided enjoyable background music for whatever we were doing. And sometimes Rachael, my older sister, who was sixteen, would sing along. Rachael had quite a pleasant voice, and both of the girls liked to play and sing 'My Blue Heaven,' which was a very popular song that year."

Owen had just turned fourteen on January 12, and he picked up some extra quarters for spending money by shoveling people's sidewalks. "Because that old North wind never seemed to stop blowing, I never ran out of work."

For many years afterward, Owen blamed himself for what occurred late one afternoon as he was shoveling snow for a neighbor. "Denise had insisted on helping me so I could get home sooner. It was several degrees below zero, and it was already dark. I will never forget how the wind sliced through our parkas. I kept a scarf over my mouth and nose so that I could breathe without the wind pushing freezing air down my lungs. Denise had forgotten to bring a scarf. I will probably always wish that I had given her mine."

Three nights later, when Denise was practicing the piano, Owen saw her pause, clear her throat, and press a hand to her chest. She had just begun to play "My Blue Heaven" when she once again pressed a hand to her chest and cried out for her mother: "Mommy, I have such an awful pain here."

Owen watched his mother rush to Denise, take her in her arms, and turn to shout at Dad, "Henry, she's burning with fever. Call Dr. Larsen."

"There's no way that he can make it here in this terrible storm," Henry Martin said, his furrowed brow expressing his anguish and frustration.

"Just call him!" His wife screamed at him as she cradled her youngest child in her arms.

Dr. Larsen told them over the telephone to put ice packs on Denise's forehead and chest until he could get there. Owen and Rachael knocked icicles off the front porch so that their mother could fashion the packs for their sister.

Owen recalled that Dr. Larsen arrived with frost on his mustache and his eyeglasses caked with a thin layer of ice. Small town legend had it that his heavy black fur coat was that of a grizzly bear that he had shot on a hunting trip to Canada. The frozen tufts of matted hair began to steam as soon as he hung it to dry in front of the coal stove.

Owen and Rachael listened outside the bedroom door as Dr. Larsen examined their sister. They heard their mother's stiffled cry of fear when the doctor cautiously diagnosed pneumonia.

"Now, now, Mrs. Martin," Dr. Larsen told her. "That fever, those chills, that sharp pain in her chest. Those symptoms are usually the first warnings of pneumonia coming on. But let's stay strong and not give in to anxiety. We'll just work hard with little Missy Denise, and we'll break that nasty congestion right out of her."

"For ten days and nights, we all did whatever

we could to save our brilliant and talented little Denise," Owen Martin stated. "We would not permit any member of the family even to think that she would not get well."

Denise herself, although trembling with terrible fever and chills, would say over and over, "I want to get well. I want to get well. I *will* get well."

Once Owen heard Denise pleading with Rachael to help her get downstairs so that she could practice the piano. "Sis," Denise sobbed, "you know I have that big recital in March. I have to practice. You must help me walk downstairs!"

Rachael would usually pacify Denise by singing "My Blue Heaven" and telling her to move her fingers on the covers as if she were playing the piano. "You can 'play' the stripes on the covers like they were piano keys and move your fingers along with my singing the words!"

It was simply not the energetic Denise's nature to lie idle in bed, regardless of how ill she might be. "Please, Mommy," she begged. "I'm going to get 'way behind on my lessons. When are you going to let me practice?"

"It won't be long, honey," Mrs. Martin said, mustering whatever shreds of optimistic conviction remained within her. "Not yet, but pretty soon."

But then Denise took a sad and pronounced turn for the worst, and the brilliant little bundle of dynamic energy and remarkable talent could only lie still in bed, trembling with fever, fighting for every breath of air that she could force into her lungs.

On that cold and awful winter's night, Dr.

Larsen moved the blankets over Denise's forever silent body. Through his grief and guilt, Owen heard the doctor say something about "edema in the lungs" having quieted his sister's talent and spirit.

A few nights after the funeral, the Martin family was seated in the frontroom at the table, trying their best to appreciate the chicken that Grandmother Jorgensen had brought over for their dinner.

"Grandma had just asked the blessing, when we heard the first notes come from the piano," Owen said. "Everyone was startled, and we all turned in our chairs to look at the keyboard. Again the notes sounded, a few bars from 'My Blue Heaven.' We all heard it as clearly as if Denise were there with us, playing the piano."

Owen's father reached out to take his wife's hand firmly in his own. "It's Denise," he said softly. "It sounds just as she would play it."

"Is . . . is it possible?" Mrs. Martin asked, tears brimming in her eyes.

Grandmother Jorgensen nodded solemnly. "Our Lord promises that we will all be joined together once again in heaven."

Once again the notes sounded from "My Blue Heaven."

"Listen," Rachael said. "Listen to the part that plays over and over. It's the part that says we will all be happy in 'my blue heaven.' "

"Is . . . is it really you, Denise?" Owen's mother cried out from the depths of her being.

The refrain sounded louder than before, then, once again, very faintly.

"Thank the blessed Lord," his mother smiled, the tears running unchecked over her cheeks. "Our little Denise is once again free to practice the piano in heaven!"

"Although we never again heard any spectral notes sound from the piano," Owen concluded, "Denise had provided each one of us with indisputable evidence of the survival of the spirit after physical death. We have all been able to lead stronger lives because of our certainty that the soul lives on and that we will one day all be listening to Denise playing for us once again—this time in heaven."

11

A Tender and Forgiving Farewell

While he was stationed in Germany in 1972, Stanley Bell met a beautiful girl named Karla Gressel with whom he enjoyed a wonderful relationship.

"In my opinion, she looked like the actress Elke Sommer—tall, blonde, almost a classic Nordic beauty," Stanley said. "We were both in our early twenties and those quaint German villages seemed made for romance. I even fantasized about staying there. I had decided upon a career in the navy, and I thought I just might chuck it all for the good life with Karla in Germany."

Stanley and Karla discussed marriage many times. "We could never quite reach a firm decision on marriage. We both said that we were in love, but whenever the topic of matrimony came up, I'm not really certain which one of us would shy away first."

Once Stanley went so far as to buy an engagement ring. "It was a beauty. It set me back mucho bucks. But I never even showed it to Karla. I guess I was afraid that she would say 'yes' and graft it to her finger forever."

When it came time for Stanley to return to the States, the two lovers were faced with the moment of truth. "We spent a last weekend together in a lovely old hotel that looked as if it had been created to be a movie set. We spent the first night virtually crying in each other's arms. We would be apart for the first time in two years. Would we ever see each other again?"

They spoke of marriage after they had made love and were slowly sipping cool glasses of Rhine wine.

"Perhaps, marriage would be fine," Karla at last spoke her inner feelings. "I can't see myself marrying anyone but you."

Stanley admitted that he felt the same way about her.

"Perhaps, then, we should see how we feel after you return to the States," Karla suggested. "Let us correspond. Let us see how we deal with the absence of one another. Let us test our love and see if we should be married."

They touched wineglasses and toasted the concept that Karla had outlined. Then they promised one another that for the remainder of the weekend they would not shed another tear over their separation, nor would they mention the word "marriage" again.

After Stanley Bell's return to the States, the two lovers continued a passionate correspondence. "For the first three or four months, I nearly went broke buying postage stamps. I wore out my thesaurus looking up synonyms for 'love,' 'passion,' and 'sweetheart.' And Karla exhibited such an uninhibited flair for writing love letters that I suggested she become a romance novelist."

Six months later, however, Stanley was finding himself concentrating more intensely on his navy career. "I had the opportunities for advancement and that meant putting my spare energy into preparing for exams, not writing love letters."

Stanley conceded that he was the first to begin to slack off on their committment to maintain an active correspondence. "I told Karla that my letters would now emphasize quality, not quantity; but pretty soon, my pace was really off. I dropped from a letter a day, to one a week, to one a month."

Karla's letters continued at a more steady pace for a few months, then she began to match his once or twice a month schedule.

"About that time I met Darcy," Stanley said. "She had been a navy brat, her father was a career man, and she really understood my love and committment for the sea. She was also gorgeous, with shoulder-length red hair, and the most incredible green eyes allowed on a human being."

Shortly after his engagement to Darcy, Stanley wrote to Karla and told her the news about his approaching marriage to another woman. "I never received an answer to my letter. I felt bad. I wondered how I would have felt if Karla had been the one to have stiffed me. But I could not help feeling that I had done the best thing for all concerned."

After his marriage, Stanley reported to duty aboard a destroyer based at the Virginia Beach, Virginia, shipyards. Darcy remained in Massachusetts while the ship was deployed to the Middle East and then passed into drydock. It was Stanley's intention to move Darcy to Virginia Beach as soon as the overhaul of the destroyer was completed.

Late on the evening of June 15, 1975, he was working in his disbursement office preparing for payday only a few days away. Stanley sat at his desk, typing up the pay roster until about 12:20 A.M.

"I had just leaned back in my chair to doze for a few minutes when I was awakened by a soft tapping at my office door. Assuming it was the security watch, I rather grouchily opened the door."

To Stanley Bell's complete and total amazement, he beheld the image of Karla Gressel, dressed only in a diaphanous light red nightgown.

"She was crying, sobbing, tears running down her cheeks. Karla looked just the way that she had the day we said good-bye in Germany."

Stanley was completley nonplussed, speechless. "At last I managed to ask her how she knew where I was and how she had been able to got aboard the destroyer without security stopping her."

She ignored Stanley's questions, but spoke

directly of other matters. "Stan, I am here to tell you that I understand about Darcy—and I forgive you."

Stanley grasped for a few words that might somehow comprise a proper response. Karla only held up her hand for silence so that she might continue.

"I was going to be married myself," she admitted. "I knew that you were right in doing what you did. My marriage was going to be very soon."

Karla took his hand in hers and held it very tightly. "I only ask one thing of you. All I want is that you will promise to remember me always with kindness."

Stanley's voice was soft, choked with emotion. "With great kindness, Karla. And with love."

"And please," she continued, "be happy, be happy in your life with Darcy."

Stanley nodded quietly, feeling tears fill the corners of his eyes.

Karla smiled, squeezed his hand in farewell, and walked quietly and quickly down the passageway until she was out of sight.

Stanley cannot estimate how long he sat quietly in reverie after Karla had left him. He does remember being roused by the security watch, who wondered if he were all right.

Stanley mumbled something that somehow satisfied the watch, then went back to work on the pay roster.

"But whatever had occurred in those incredible few moments in the flow of my normal life experience had blown me away," he stated. "There was no way that I could remove the incident from my mind. To try to sell myself on the concept that I had dozed off and had a vivid dream was out of the question. I knew that I had seen Karla with my wakeful senses."

Stanley set aside his paperwork and wrote a letter to Karla, detailing his remarkable experience and asking her if she were all right. "I wanted to know if she might be ill, or if she might have been thinking intently of me at the time that her image had appeared in my office aboard the destroyer."

A few weeks later, Stanley received a reply from Mrs. Rolf Gressel, Karla's mother, who informed him that Karla had died instantly in a head-on autmoble crash early in the morning of June 16. The time of Karla's death was equivalent to about 12:20 A.M. June 15 in Virginia Beach.

"Mrs. Gressel told me that she had been looking for my address to inform me of her daughter's death just as my letter arrived," Stanley said. "Only days before Karla's fatal accident, she had spoken of me and said how sorry she was that she had not answered my letter about my marriage to Darcy. Mrs. Gressel also verified that Karla was engaged to be married at the time of her death. The bond of love that we had once shared had somehow enabled her to bid me a tender and forgiving farewell."

12

We Are Always One
Throughout Eternity

After Edythe Burns lost her husband, Oliver, the uncanny sensation that he was still with her persisted. He made his presence known by the little things that had meant so much to her when he was still alive. There would be a touch on her shoulder now and then . . . a caress on her hair . . . a tender brush against her cheek.

Oliver had died at the age of 68 after a long illness. He had been an avid reader and writer of poetry and had managed to see a number of his poems published in periodicals and journals. Because he had been a junior college football coach until he retired, people always seemed surprised when they discovered his avocation. The local newspaper had even done a feature on him some years back when it became known that one of his poems was to be published in a national magazine. "From Pigskin to Poetry" the headline over the story declared.

Oliver had been dead for nine months when Edythe experienced a strange and beautiful mystical connection with his spirit. "I was really feeling low, in the very depths of despair," she said. "I missed Oliver so much. My life no longer seemed to have any purpose, any meaning. I had awakened from a terrible dream in which I seemed to be all alone in the world. Our only son lived in Germany at that time. He had come home for the funeral, but his work made it difficult to visit the States often. I began to feel so overcome by loneliness that I was seized by a spasm of uncontrolled weeping, and I began to yearn to see my own life come to an end."

Suddenly, Edythe remembered, she sensed a presence at her bedside. "I looked up to see a dimly lighted outline of a form that I knew to be Oliver's. I could almost, but not quite, distinguish his features."

Her immediate startled response quickly faded as she watched the illuminated form begin to move over her own body. "The glowing, mistlike image began to lower itself to me, and I felt the most incredible sensation as Oliver's light body blended with my physical body. Never before on the material plane had I felt so at one with him. That night we truly became one flesh, one spirit, one entity of love."

The sense of total oneness with her husband's spirit lasted for what seemed to be nearly an hour. After the experience had ended, she was blessed with a wonderful peace, and she drifted into a deep and dreamless sleep.

"I never again felt loneliness or despair," Edythe said. "Oliver returned that night to prove to me that we will always be one throughout eternity."

13

His Father Proved That
Life Is Forever

Herb Cutner and his father, Bob, used to sit up half the night discussing the possibility of life after death. The elder Cutner was a strong believer in the continuation of the human personality beyond the grave, but Herb was not so certain.

"Dad had been raised a strict Baptist and there probably never was a time in his life when he did not believe in the existence of the soul and its promise of life eternal," Herb said. "Although he was still a regular churchgoer, he had in his later years begun to explore the world of psychical research and said that he found many proofs of life after death in the scientific approach of modern parapsychologists. It wasn't that I really *disbelieved* in life after death. It was just that I didn't believe completely enough to satisfy my father."

Then, in the fall of 1969, when Herb was 13 years old, he was awakened at 3:30 A.M. by loud rapping noises coming from the guest room.

"I remember being seized by a primitive sense of fear," he recalled. "I was admittedly frightened, and I remained in bed until I heard my dad coming up the stairs from his bedroom downstairs. Secure in his presence, I joined him in the guest room and asked him what he thought was making the peculiar rapping sounds. He laughed it off and assured me that it was nothing more than the furnace kicking in against the autumn chill."

But that afternoon, Herb stated, his father received word that his sister Harriet had passed away at 3:30 that morning. "Aunt Harriet had always stayed in our guest room whenever she came to visit," Herb said. "She always told us how much she liked the room, how pleasant she found it to be. Dad, Mom, my sister Debbie, and I openly discussed the rappings that had sounded at the moment of her death, and we accepted them as Aunt Harriet's having made contact with us at the moment of her death."

Herb had received acceptable proof that the spirit survives physical death, and from that time on, he was able to discuss psychical research with his father on a much freer basis.

Herb had nearly forgotten about the mysterious rappings until nearly eighteen years later when a loud crash jolted him out of a deep sleep on September 27, 1987.

"I sat up and listened, but I could hear no other strange sounds emanating from any corner of our apartment," Herb said. "The only discernible sounds were the steady breathing of my wife Luana sleeping beside me and the low purr of the refrigerator in the kitchen. I kept thinking that the sound had come from our closet, that something must have toppled over and crashed to the floor. Finding no evidence of such a fall, I assumed that I had been dreaming, I lay back down and dozed off."

Herb had hardly nestled back into sleep when a loud rapping sound began. This time he was certain that the raps were issuing from the closet.

"As soon as I would sit up, the rapping would cease. When I lay back down, they would begin again, seemingly more loudly than before," Herb said.

"What's making that weird noise?" Luana asked, no longer able to sleep through the persistent rapping. "It seems to be coming from the closet."

The two of them went to investigate, turning on the light, moving boxes, examining Herb's heavy hiking shoes.

"Something was pounding somewhere in this apartment," Luana said adamantly. "I'm going to keep looking until I find out what it was."

Herb and Luana searched their entire apartment in vain. "Nothing was out of the ordinary. So at last, at four o'clock in the morning, we crawled back in bed, determined to catch a few more winks before the alarm went off at six."

They had barely sighed their "good mornings" to each other when the rappings started again.

"That's when I remembered about Aunt Harriet and the rappings in the guest room back home," Herb said. "The moment I said aloud, 'Oh, my God! It's like when Aunt Harriet's spirit rapped on the guest room walls,' the noises ceased."

Luana put her arms around him. "Oh, honey," she hesitated, picking her words carefully. "Could it be . . . your dad? You've been so concerned about his heart problems."

Herb had been struggling with the same uncomfortable question. His father had been suffering from a steadily weakening heart condition for the past several years.

"I know it can't be Dad," he said, as much to reassure himself. "He's on a fishing trip up north with some of his old buddies. You know how sensible Dad is. He wouldn't have gone on the trip if his heart had been bothering him."

Luana nodded. "I guess so. Besides, one of his friends would have called your mom if anything had happened to Dad."

To calm both of their nerves, however, Herb decided to wait an hour and call his mother. With the hour difference in time zones, he knew that she would be up and awake by then.

"Dad's fine," she assured them. "He phoned late last night to tell me that he would be home this afternoon as planned."

Nevertheless, Herb was not really surprised when his mother called him at work later that day to share the sad news that Dad had suffered a major heart attack that morning and had died on the way to a hospital. The official time of death was registered as 10:45 A.M.

"I know that one level of Dad's consciousness had contacted me just a few hours prior to his death in order to prepare me for the shock of his passing," Herb said. "But the proofs of survival presented to his family by my believing father did not end there."

Herb and Luana flew home for the funeral and were faced with the unpleasant task of finding a place for Bob Cutner's internment. "Dad had never purchased a burial plot, and Mom was extremely distraught because she had no idea of where Dad would like to be buried."

Herb had been away from home for several years, so he just suggested the first cemetery that came to his memory, and the three of them drove out to speak to a salesperson.

"Because Dad had been such a nature lover, we wanted to purchase a burial plot near trees, but the salesman told us that he was sorry but the only areas remaining unsold were those in the fields, quite some distance away from any trees. Mom begged him to check his files one more time.

"The salesman thumbed through a thick sheaf of papers, shook his head slowly, expressing his apology that no such plot under trees remained. Then, while reaching for a map indicating the available areas, he found a notice of cancellation on a plot with trees whose owners had moved out of state.

"In amazement," Herb said, "we all saw that the cancellation had been made at 10:45 on the day that Dad had died. And the plot sounded beautiful, right under a beautiful oak tree. We asked to see it immediately."

As they drove to the site, the salesman remarked

how peculiar it was that the previous owners had cancelled so conveniently for the Cutners—especially since they had moved from the city over a year earlier.

While his mother and Luana stood silently reflecting over the grave plot, Herb wandered pensively in the area, idly reading the names on the nearby tombstones.

"I was suddenly startled to read 'William Cutner' on a tombstone," Herb said. "Dad had grown up in Wisconsin and had very few relatives in the area. His brother had been one of them, but he had died when he was only a teenager, quite a few years before Dad and Mom were married. Neither Mom nor I knew where Uncle William had been buried. Now I had just discovered his grave, three plots away from the one that we were buying for Dad."

The comforting proofs of spirit survival that Bob Cutner had orchestrated for his family from beyond the grave were not yet completed.

When Herb, his mother, and Luana arrived back at the family home, they found that his sister Debbie had arrived with her husband and children. Debbie's eyes were red from weeping, but she greeted them with a smile of unparalleled joy.

She told them that shortly after she had heard the news of Dad's death, she had gone into their living room to sit beneath a painting that Dad had given her for Christmas several years before.

"It's the picture of Jesus standing at the door, knocking to be admitted," she reminded them. "Since Dad had one like it and I knew it meant so much to him, I sat beneath it, praying for comfort, praying for some sign of Dad's spiritual ascension."

After only a few moments in prayer, Debbie had been startled when the painting had fallen off the wall. As she picked it up to replace it, she saw a sheet of Dad's familiar stationery between the glass and the backing of the frame. It was a note from Dad, which Debbie shared with the family:

"To my dear children: No matter where I am, I will always be with you. I will always love you—whether in this life or in the next. Love, Dad."

Bob Cutner had given his family the most precious gift imaginable. He had provided them with an unshakable faith in life after death.

14

Her Husband's Spirit Is Always Watching Over Them

The diagnosis that James' illness would be fatal was pronounced so suddenly that Margaret Stevens did not have enough time to adjust either psychologically or emotionally to her husband's impending death. It seemed as though one day they were discussing where they would vacation and whether or not to open a special savings account for their twelve-year-old daughter's future college education—and the next they were awkwardly and painfully attempting to plan for her life without Jim.

In those moments when the awful reality of rapidly approaching hurt and loss permitted her a more dispassionate assessment of her situation, Margaret would console herself with the recognition that she and Jim had enjoyed nearly twenty years of a very happy marriage. By combining their two salaries, they had been able to provide themselves with the basic necessities and with enough of the extras that made their lives complete. They frugally planned and spaced the births of their two children (Dorothy, age twelve and David, age nine). They played tennis together, jogged together in rain or sunshine, enjoyed a little conservative dabbling in the stockmarket. Surely, even the most critical gossips in the medium-sized Missouri city where they lived would have to admit that they had always been a nearly perfect couple.

On June 22, Jim had fainted after their afternoon tennis set. Two days later in the office of their family doctor, they sat together holding hands while Dr. Lucas solemnly told them that Jim had only a few weeks to live. Dr. Lucas cried along with them. He had known both of them since they were teenagers. He had delivered both Dorothy and David.

Six weeks later, on a hot August night, Jim lay in a coma in the county hospital. Around ten o'clock, Dr. Lucas informed Margaret that the end was near.

"There's nothing more you can do here, Maggie," the doctor advised her. "Why don't you go on home for a while and try to get some rest?"

Margaret blinked back the tears. Dr. Lucas was so kind, just like Luke, the Beloved Physician, one of Jesus' disciples. She knew that he was thinking of her welfare, but she could not leave Jim alone.

"You know that I've got to be there at Jim's bedside," Margaret said, trying her best not to cry. "What if he should come out of the coma for even a moment or two and not find me there at his side? And since we moved to that place out in the country, it's just too far to drive home only to come back if he needs me."

Dr. Lucas put an arm lightly across her shoulders and brought her trembling body next to his solid frame. "Maggie, Jim has been unconscious for days. Look at yourself. You're right on the brink of exhaustion. What good can you be to Dorothy and David if you end up sick and in the hospital yourself?"

Margaret started to bring up the problem of the distance between home and hospital, but Dr. Lucas interrupted her with the suggestion that she get a room in Mitch Snyder's motel near the hospital.

"Let the front desk know your room number as soon as you've registered," he said. "I promise to call you if there is any change in Jim's condition."

A large window in the hospital lobby had been given a mirrorlike quality by the night's darkness and Margaret caught a glimpse of herself. Her red-rimmed eyes looked deep-set because of the dark circles beneath them. Her hair was unkempt, disarrayed. Her face was puffy from crying, wan from lack of sleep. Perhaps Dr. Lucas was right. She had better get some rest.

For over an hour she had sat on the edge of the bed in the motel room, reading passages from the Gideon Bible that she remembered had to do with the eternality of the soul and of the promise of the resurrection. She and Jim were members of the Methodist congregation in their community, and while they might not have been the most faithful in regular church attendance, she had always been a student of the Bible.

Margaret lay beneath sheets that were surprisingly crisp considering the high humidity of that steamy August night. Around 2:00 A.M. she shut off the bedside lamp in the hope that the drone of the air-conditioner might lull her to sleep.

She did fall asleep almost at once, but she began to dream of the first time that she had met Jim. They were both seventeen, and he was transferring schools. He was a big city boy from St. Louis, and he had been arrogantly contemptuous of small town girls. It hadn't taken her long to set him right, though.

Margaret's dream machinery flashed a montage of images—the junior-senior prom, their wedding, the car crash that totaled their new Ford, the births of Dorothy and David.

She awakened in tears at 2:24. She had dreamed bits and pieces of their entire loving relationship in a matter of minutes. From that time on, she dozed fitfully, awakening to check the bedside clock-radio every fifteen or twenty minutes.

Then, strangely, at exactly 4:28 A.M., Margaret Stevens sensed a familiar presence. "Jim," she whispered, as she turned over on her back and sat up in bed.

She could see her husband clearly in the dim light of the motel room. Somehow, in a manner that she would never be able to understand completely, Jim stood at the bed-side.

"I am leaving you now, baby," Jim said, his voice full and rich, as it had been before the terrible illness had wasted his strength, his body, even the timbre of his speech. "This fleshly shell that I have been using is no longer of any use to me. I am sad to be leaving you, honey, but don't worry. I'll always be there watching over you and the kids."

Margaret sat motionless long after the image of her husband had faded from the room. She was convinced that Jim had died and that his spirit had come to say good-bye to her.

Somehow—although she later marveled at the fact—grief was unable to penetrate the dazed mental condition created by the sudden appearance of her husband's spirit. The part of her brain that was still thinking, still functioning, kept awaiting the hospital's call that would inform her of Jim's death.

The call did not come until 9:00 A.M., nearly five hours after Jim's apparition had appeared to her.

Later, after she had taken care of some details at the hospital, she wanted to speak with the attending physician at the time of Jim's death. As Margaret expected, Dr. Lucas was off-duty, at home resting, so she asked to see Dr. Montgomery, her husband's ward doctor. When the physician asked in a polite and businesslike manner if there was something that he might do for her, she asked if she could see Jim's chart.

"I'm sorry, Mrs. Stevens," he told her. "That is highly irregular and against hospital rules."

He was about to continue his mechanical recitation of hospital regulations when there was something in Margaret Stevens' manner that cut him short. "*Why* do you wish to see your husband's chart, Mrs. Stevens?"

Margaret prayed for the inner strength to sound coherent. "I would like very much . . . it is very important to me to verify the exact time of my husband's death. I . . . I have a strong conviction that Jim died at 4:28 A.M., even though the hospital staff and Dr. Lucas promised to call me if Jim awakened or if there were any change in his condition."

"And when were you called?" Dr. Montgomery wanted to know.

"Not until 9:00 A.M."

The physician appeared ready to continue with his recitation of hospital policy.

"Please, Dr. Montgomery," Margaret said softly, tears warping her voice. "It is very important to me to know this . . . to know exactly what time Jim died."

The physician called to a nurse seated at a desk to bring James Stevens' chart. When he had it in his hand, his eyebrows raised, and he showed it to Margaret, his forefinger pointing to the time of death—4:28 A.M.

Margaret Stevens' eyes brimmed with tears. She had not been dreaming. Jim had appeared to her at the moment of his death.

Her beloved husband had come to bid her good-bye, to give evidence of his undying love for her, and to offer dramatic proof of the human personality's ability to surive the experience of physical death.

As she turned to leave the ward, the nurse touched her gently on the arm. "Don't be too hard on Dr. Lucas. Your husband never regained consciousness, and the doctor thought you really needed your rest."

Margaret managed to smile and to nod her understanding.

"But you knew, didn't you?" the nurse asked her. "Somehow you knew the precise moment when your husband's soul left his body."

"I knew," Margaret whispered, then found herself unable to speak further in her deep emotion.

"Someday," the nurse said, "I pray that I might experience my own proof of the soul's survival after death."

15

A Spirit Removed Her
Wedding Ring

Lorraine Thomason used to tease her husband that their marriage would have to last forever, because her wedding ring was so tight that she would never be able to get it off her finger.

"And that's the way it'll stay until I tell you differently," Lyle would always answer her with a chuckle.

There were few things to laugh and to tease about in 1943, especially if one were the wife of a serviceman. Lorraine and Lyle had had their first argument when he enlisted in the army.

"You can barely find your nose to blow it without your glasses," she snapped angrily when she found out that he would soon be leaving on a bus for basic training. "You were declared 4-F because of your bad eyesight. Did you bribe the draftboard?"

"Things are getting tough over there, pumpkin," Lyle tried to explain. "They think that maybe now my eyes aren't so bad. They need men to win this war."

"You just aren't really happy with me," Lorraine accused him. "You just want to get away from me!"

She regretted at once having said such a thing. First of all, she knew it wasn't true. Secondly, if it *were* true, she surely shouldn't have said the terrible words out loud so Lyle could agree with them.

"You know that's not true," Lyle reassured her. "But how can a fella stay home and dance with his wife to Glenn Miller records when some of his best friends, guys he grew up with, are getting killed and chopped up?"

She knew that he was referring to Skinny Horwitz who had been killed in Italy and to Art Minaldi who had stepped on a landmine and been sent home without his legs. She also knew that there was no use to argue about it. She would have to join the ranks of the G.I. wives and grin and bear it.

In November of that year, Lyle was shipped overseas to the European theater of action, and Lorraine decided to leave the city and live with his parents on their old farm homestead in New Hampshire. Ed and Mary Thomason treated their daughter-in-law with warmth and consideration, and they gave her Lyle's old room, complete with its own stone fireplace. Each night at dusk, Mrs. Melvina Thomason, Ed's mother, would build a

roaring fire on the grate, and in the morning
she would revive the cherry-red coals with fresh
wood. All in all, Lorraine had to admit, it was
pretty much an idyllic existence—except that Lyle
wasn't there with her.

The progress of the war in Europe domi-
nated nearly every dinnertime conversation. Ed
had a habit of reading aloud from the newspaper after the evening meal. Later, his news
reporting would be supplemented by the war
correspondents' dispatches on the radio. By mid-
January, 1945, things were going badly for the
Allies. The Nazis seemed to sense that they
were losing the war, and they were determined
to make the Allies pay dearly for their victo-
ry.

Letters from Lyle arrived only sporadically, and
they were filled with his longing to return home.
It seemed to Lorraine as though she could feel
the deep emotion of his love and his sorrow, and
sometimes she would press them close to her chest,
as if she could somehow link up their very heart
beats.

In February, 1945, a letter from Lyle arrived,
and Lorraine read it aloud to his parents and
Grandmother Thomason. Although censorship
requirements would not allow him to be specific,
Lyle wrote in general terms about preparations
for a major offensive.

Two nights after she had received the letter
from her husband, Lorraine remembered going
to sleep filled with prayerful concern for Lyle's
safety. "I prayed for hours," she recalled. "Then I

fell asleep watching the flames swirl up the stone chimney."

She awakened sometime that night, her entire being suffused with terrible cold. "I felt cold and clammy clear to my very bones. I sat up in bed to see if the fire had gone out, and I saw Lyle standing there."

Lorraine remembered that her husband's features were clearly distinguishable in the red glow of the fireplace. "He looked tired and sad. He just stared at me for the longest time, then he walked over to the bed, leaned over me, and took my hand. I felt tears spring to my eyes as Lyle gently slipped my wedding ring off my finger. I'll never forget how cold his hands felt. He opened his mouth as if he were going to speak to me—then he disappeared."

Lorraine shook her head, then closed her eyes and rubbed them with the palms of her hands. When she opened her eyes again, she found reassurance in the reality of the room's familiar fixtures. It had all been a dream.

The fire in the grate was very low. It would soon be morning. She pulled the heavy quilts over her shivering frame and lay in silence until she heard the morning sounds of the Thomason family shaking off sleep. When she was certain that everyone was up and assembled in the kitchen for breakfast, she came out to tell them of her strange dream of Lyle.

"That was no dream," Grandmother Thomason pronounced after Lorraine had completed her account. "Our poor Lyle is dead," she concluded, shaking her head wisely.

Lorraine protested. It had only been a dream, nothing more.

"Then where is your wedding ring?" Grandmother wanted to know. "Where is that ring that none of us have ever seen you remove? Where is that ring that Lyle said could never come off unless he took it off himself?"

Lorraine clutched her hands together as if she could somehow prevent the ring's escape. She knew that she had purposely avoided looking at her ring finger, and now she was forced to regard the finger for the first time since she had awakened. She was startled to see that it no longer bore the wedding band that had so tightly encircled it.

They found the wedding ring on the dresser in her room, but Lorraine could offer no explanation of how the snug band could have been removed from her finger.

Grandmother Thomason insisted that the explanation had already been told: The spirit of Lyle had removed it when he had come to say good-bye.

A bit too sharply, Ed demanded that his mother cease such talk. In his opinion, Lorraine had suffered a bad dream that had been caused by her natural wifely concern for a husband who was off fighting a war. She wouldn't be the first person who walked in her sleep and who managed to do something in the dream state that she could not easily accomplish in the waking state.

Lorraine had immediately replaced the ring on her finger. On one level of consciousness, she knew that Grandmother Thomason was correct in her interpretation of the strange events. Although she refused to permit the thought complete expression, Lorraine somehow knew that the spiritual essence of Lyle had come to say good-bye. The removal of their wedding band symbolized the termination of their earthly bond.

Two weeks later a telegram arrived from the War Department informing them of Lyle Thomason's death in military action. Lyle had been killed on February 8. His spirit image had appeared to Lorraine shortly after that, on February 9.

Lorraine Thomason eventually remarried, but she has never forgotten the bond of love that managed to transmit the image of her dying husband over thousands of miles to appear before her in her bedroom. She has listened to others explain the phenomenon of the apparition of Lyle removing the tight ring from her finger by suggesting that she herself removed it in a kind of trance state after receiving a telepathic impression of her husband's death.

"I cannot accept such an explanation," she stated firmly. "When Lyle's ghost touched the ring, it literally slipped off my finger. I couldn't even get it off with warm soapy water. My finger would just start to swell, and I couldn't budge it."

For many years, she admitted, she considered Lyle's spirit as a sort of guardian angel.

"Somehow I always knew that he was up there looking after me. I did not date at all for five years after Lyle's death. I almost married one fellow, but I felt that Lyle strongly disapproved of him. I definitely sensed a greenlight with Al, my present husband, though."

16

The Mystery of the "Old Lady" Who Knocked Father Down

Although Karen Jelinek knew that her father had hardening of the arteries and often became mentally confused, she was terribly annoyed when he had referred to her mother as "that old lady" when she died.

Her parents, Karl and Lara Kappas, had been out for a walk in the small park above their home when Lara had suffered a sudden stroke and had fallen to the sidewalk. Karl had been leaning heavily on his cane with one hand and resting his arm on his wife when she had made a gasping sound and collapsed. Karl had also been carried to the ground by the force of her fall, and the two elderly people had been found on the sidewalk, pitifully intertwined.

Lara Kappas had died without regaining consciousness, and Karl had been brought home to the residence of his daughter, Mrs. Karen Jelinek, seemingly more confused than ever.

"Lara was dying and leaving me," he told Karen with tears coursing down his cheeks. "I wanted to talk with her longer, but that old lady crashed into me and we both fell to the sidewalk. How I wish that she hadn't knocked me down just then."

Karen was so shattered by the loss of her mother that she found it difficult to be patient with her father. He seemed to be concerned only that his wife had knocked into him and they had both fallen to the sidewalk. And it offended her that he kept referring to her mother as "that old lady."

Karen resolved to be as compassionate as possible, and for several months she simply tuned out whatever her father had to say about her mother's death. Then one day he said something that made her listen to his mumbled monologue with greater interest.

"I wonder," he said, staring thoughtfully into the space before him. "I wonder if that old lady died, too?"

What did he mean when he wondered if *she* died, *too*?

"Dad," Karen asked softly. "Tell me again how Mother died."

Her father squeezed the curved handle of his cane until his knuckles stood out like white marbles. Tears gathered in the corner of his eyes. He took a deep breath, emitted a gentle sigh.

"We were walking in the park, like we always loved to do," Karl Kappas began. "Then, Lara, your mother, stopped me and said that she was sorry, but that it was time for her to go . . . to die. I begged her not to leave me, but she left my side and began to walk down the hill toward the pond where the swans swim.

"A golden shaft of light came down from the sky, and two tall men in flowing robes stepped forward to take Lara by the hand. I called to her again, and she turned as if to tell me goodbye.

"But," Karl said, his voice cracking with sorrow, "I never heard what she said . . . because that was when that old lady stumbled into me . . . and knocked me down."

For the first time Karen realized that her father had not associated Lara, her mother, with the "old lady" who had pulled him down with her to the sidewalk. Upon further questioning, Karen discovered that, in his mental confusion, her father had seen his wife as she appeared when she was much younger. The apparition that had come to tell him farewell was an image of his Lara in the full bloom of her womanhood, not the plump, wrinkled gray-haired "old lady" who had knocked him down at such an inopportune moment.

17

Ghosts of the Living

"Also when they shall be afraid of that which is high, and fears shall be in the way, and the almond tree shall flourish and the grasshopper shall be a burden, and desire shall fail; because man goeth to his long home, and the mourners go about the streets. Or ever the silver cord be loosed, or the golden bowl be broken, or the pitcher be broken at the fountain, or the wheel be broken at the cistern. Then shall the dust return to the earth as it was: and the spirit shall return to God who gave it." *Ecclesiastes*, 12:5–7.

The biblical reference quoted above is often given as scriptural testimony of the reality of the spiritual body within each of us and of our ability to separate spirit from flesh and to soar apart from all physical considerations. Many of those men and women who have undergone near-death experiences (NDE) or out-of-body experiences (OBE) have reported seeing themselves as "golden bowls," or globular spheres of some sort, and just as many have seen a "silver cord" of great elasticity which connects the spirit body to the physical body. Although the spirit body may sometimes assume a form that exactly duplicates the physical body, generally both the metaphysicians, who have been speaking about spirit bodies for centuries, and those who have had a one-time, spontaneous NDE or OBE describe the spirit body as being more or less egg-shaped with an orange glow—the "golden bowl" of scripture.

The spirit body is sometimes referred to as the "astral body" or the "second body," and in his book *You Do Take It With You*, R. De Witt Miller emphatically states his acceptance of such an ethereal aspect of humankind to explain a host of psychic phenomena.

Miller writes that present day physics has demonstrated that the desk top or table top that seems perfectly solid to our fingers is actually composed of atoms, which in turn are composed of nuclei and electrons. Since nuclei are considered as composed of many distinct types of particles, the desk before us is *solid* only in the sense that it seems solid to the sensory organs with which our fingertips are equipped. In reality, the *solid* desk top is largely made up of what, for lack of a more precise word, is usually referred to as "empty space."

Miller goes on to theorize that just as there is no reason why empty space should not be occupied by another form of matter or conventional matter at a different rate of vibration, there is no reason why the physical body of a human could not be "interpenetrated" with a second body composed of a different form of matter or existing in a different range of vibration.

"The desk top," Miller makes note, "would not be solid to such a body, but objects in the world to which that body belongs would be."

Writing just a bit before the concept of the atom became a serious addition to modern physics, Sylvan Muldoon, an author of several classic books on out-of-body experience, also known as "astral projection," tried to explain his idea of the astral body by telling his reader to take an ordinary glass tumbler and fill it to the brim with round lead pellets. When this was accomplished, Muldoon pointed out, it was still quite possible to pour in a good amount of birdshot, which would filter into the intervening spaces without really making the glass any "fuller." After the birdshot, one might pour in a good amount of sand; and finally, water might be added before the glass might truly be said to be "full."

"What all this amounts to is really this," Muldoon explained in *The Case for Projection of the Astral Body*. "That between all particles of matter there is still room for still smaller particles, which fill the spaces between them. So far as we can see, this is true of everything down to the atoms themselves."

If Muldoon had written the above a few years later, he would have had the advantage of knowing that even the atoms themselves are full of "holes." Can we say, then, that the "holes" in our physical body may be filled with the stuff of a much more subtle body—a spirit body?

The great psychical researcher Frederic W. H. Myers once referred to astral projection and accounts of out-of-body experiences as the most extraordinary achievement of the human will. In his *Human Personality and Its Survival of Bodily Death*, he commented: "What can lie further outside any known capacity than the power to cause a semblance of oneself to appear at a distance?" Myers asked. "What can be more a central action—more manifestly the outcome of whatsoever is deepest and most unitary in man's whole being?

"Of all vital phenomena, I say this is the most significant; this self-projection is the one definite act which it seems as though a man might perform equally well before and after bodily death."

We totally agree that accounts of "ghosts of the living," such as the report of Pat Mehan that follows, offer most convincing proof that we each have within us a spirit body that exists as our essential vehicle of individual expression *both before and after bodily death*.

Pat Mehan was alone in a fourteen-foot trench, welding some new water pipes for a soon-to-open housing development in a large New England city. It is quite unlikely that Pat had ever given the slightest thought to any sort of spiritual experience, and if anyone had told him about the possibility that he might travel in the spirit, independent of the body, he would have laughed in his face.

Pat Mehan had a wife and six kids to support. He worked on a city maintenance crew from 6:30 A.M. to 4:00 P.M. and had a second job as a garage attendant from 8:00 P.M. until midnight. He went to mass on Sunday whenever he could—Christmas and Easter for certain—but he had no time at all for metaphysical speculation.

Then on a late afternoon in the spring of 1965, Pat Mehan was given a most dramatic, albeit painful, demonstration that he had within himself remarkable resources which lie ready to serve him in crisis situations.

By 3:30 P.M., the power-shovel crew had laid the last pipe in place for the day. At 4:00 P.M. the crew knocked off work for the day, but Mehan did not have to report for work at the garage that night, so he decided to pick up some overtime by finishing the welding on the seam between the last two pipes in the trench.

He had finished his work on the inside seam and was about to begin on the outside of the joint when tons of earth, clay, and stones caved in around and upon him. He had absolutely no warning of any kind. The trench caved in silently, as if it had planned to trap him.

He was knocked down in a kneeling position against the big pipe. His nose was crunched up against the plate of the welding mask.

For a few moments, he was conscious of searing pain as his right shoulder was pressed against the hot weld he had been making on the pipes. In agony, he tried desperately to squirm away from the burning pipe, but the press of the cave-in held his shoulder against the red-hot weld.

He tried to twist his face free of the welding mask, then realized that it had saved his life. Without the pocket which the mask had made around his face, the loose dirt would have covered his nose and mouth and he would soon have suffocated.

Pat Mehan lay still, taking stock of his situation.

He had been covered by a cave-in in a trench in a new housing district. *That was certainly a negative!*

His crew had gone home. He was all alone. *Another big negative!*

No construction workers or carpenters were working on this side of the district (*Negative*), but (*Positive*) there was a slim chance that some of them might have occasion to walk by the trench and see the cave-in.

But *how* would they see him? Mehan swallowed hard, reluctantly eliminating his one slim positive factor. The terrible realizaton that there was no one to come to his rescue dug into his consciousness and began to slice away at the thin mental barrrier that had saved him from immediate panic.

Then he realized that his right hand was sticking up through the dirt!

Somehow, when the force of the cave-in had struck him, his right shoulder had been pressed forward against the hot weld and his right arm had been straightened back and above his body, thus allowing his hand to remain above the surface, free to wave like a lonely five-fingered flag. His hand could be his salvation.

Time quickly became a concept devoid of all meaning. Had he been there hours, days, weeks, months? *How long really?* Perhaps ten minutes. Maybe only five.

Already it was becoming difficult to breathe—very difficult. He had been fortunate in that he had been forced up against the large pipe, thereby creating air pockets near him.

But the blood from his broken nose kept dripping into his throat, and he feared that he would soon choke and strangle on it. He was sickened by the thought of drowning in his own blood.

Would no one ever come by?

Pat Mehan thought of his wife, his children, and he was startled by the vividness of the images that came before his mental viewing screen. It truly seemed as if each member of his family had suddenly entered into the terrible trench to be with him in his anguish.

"The more I thought about my family," Mehan remembered, "the more I wanted to be with them. Each breath that I was taking was beginning to feel like hot lead being forced down my nostrils. The next thing I knew, I seemed to be floating above the trench. I figure now that I fainted, but then I thought that I had died.

"I could see my hand kind of drooping down over a bit of my wrist sticking above the dirt. I didn't really seem to care about what had happened to me. I didn't feel sad.

"Then I thought of my family, and just like that, I was there in the kitchen of my home. My wife Clarice was peeling potatoes for the evening meal. Katie, my oldest girl, was helping her. I walked through the house and saw each one of the kids. Some were watching television. Others were doing homework. I wanted to hug them one last time. I wanted them to see me. That's when I felt sad. That's when I knew that I didn't want to die. I had found out that it wasn't really painful to die, but I just didn't want to leave the wife and the kids.

"I seemed to float into the kitchen, and I got up right next to my wife's shoulder, and I tried to scream in her ear that I needed help. She couldn't hear me.

"I reached out to touch her, and whether it was coincidence or what, she jerked around with a surprised look on her face. But I just couldn't get through to her.

"Then, for some reason, I thought of my best friend, B. J. Murphy, who was also a welder. I no sooner pictured him in my mind than I was there beside him. I could see his wristwatch, because he had his shirt sleeves rolled up. It was 4:45, which meant that I had been in the caved-in trench about fifteen minutes. B. J. works for a commercial firm, not the city, and he would be working until five o'clock, or after, depending on the job.

"Welding work becomes kind of automatic after a while, so B. J. was standing there, welding away, not really thinking about much of anything. I could actually see certain things that he was thinking, and his thoughts were all jumbled up, like in a dream. I suppose he was kind of daydreaming, and maybe that's how I was able to get through to him.

"I tapped him on the shoulder, and he shut off the torch and lifted up his face mask. I thought just as hard as I could: 'B. J.! I need your help!'

"His eyes opened wide, like he had seen a ghost. And I guess he had. Me. He said my name just once in a hoarse voice.

"Oscar Thorson, who was working with him, asked him who he was talking to, and B. J. said that he thought he had seen me standing in front of him.

"Oscar said that B. J. must be seeing things, and I thought, 'Oh, dear God, please make Oscar shut up and please help B. J. to come to me.'

"The next thing I knew, I felt some hands pulling at me, and I could hear a lot of excited voices. Above all the noise, I could hear B. J. telling everyone to take it easy with me.

"At first I was still confused. I didn't really know for certain if I was still floating around like some ghost, or if I was really back in my physical body. I felt scared right away, because I thought that maybe my mind was just playing tricks with me and that now I really *was* dead. Then a wonderful kind of peace came over me, and when I woke up again, I was in the hospital and all my family was standing around me."

Pat Mehan was greatly impressed with the authenticity of his experience. He had never been concerned with spiritual phenomena, nor had he ever read any literature that dealt with psychic experiences. Now he is convinced that he and his mind are more than physical things.

His friend B. J. Murphy was quite vocal concerning his side of the experience. When he looked up from his welding, he had at first thought that his eyes had not yet adjusted from dealing with the bright glare of the welding torch. Although a welder wears a tinted face plate in his helmet, he is still very susceptible to after-images from such work. When B. J. was convinced that his eyes were not playing tricks on him, he was certain that he could distinguish a misty outline of his friend Pat Mehan standing before him. B. J. had also received a very strong sense of danger, and he was motivated to leave his work and to drive to the housing development where he knew that Pat Mehan was working with his crew. Although B. J. knew that his friend should have ceased working nearly an hour before, he also *knew* that Pat was still there and needed his help.

B. J. Murphy has had a number of experiences he considers to have been paranormal in nature. He believes firmly in the immortality of the soul and is convinced that there is within humankind a spiritual essence that survives physical death. B. J. had a prior experience similar to that of perceiving the "living ghost" of Pat Mehan when his sister appeared to him at the moment of her death.

It would appear, then, that B. J. served as just precisely the proper receiver for Pat Mehan's telepathic cry for help from his spirit body. Mehan was indeed most fortunate to have a friend who was so readily able to "tune in" and to rescue him.

18

Her "Real Self" Was Rolled Up in a Corner of the Room

Mary Wollman had always had an aversion to drugs. And so even after surgery, and in spite of her physician's instructions to flash the nurse when the numbing effects of the "hypo" wore off, she refused to call for the blissful relief of another hypodermic injection.

Just at the point of intense pain (she was about to yield to the doctor's instructions and reach for the bulb by her pillow to flash for the nurse), Mary began to experience an odd sensation: "It was as if my feet, my legs, my body were being rolled up like a giant toothpaste tube. Then my *real* self seemed to be all rolled up in a corner of my skull. There was a really intense spasm of pain, and then I seemed to shoot up into a corner of the room.

"I thought I'd died. For a fleeting moment, I felt upset and angered at the injustice of dying as the result of such minor surgery," she recalled. "I morosely attributed my death to the inadequacies of the hospital staff and the incompetence of my doctor. Then a warm wave of peace seemed to wash over me, and I thought how foolish it was to care about a continued existence in that painfully throbbing shell that lay stretched out on the hospital bed.

"From my peculiar vantage point up in a corner of the room, I had a unique opportunity to observe myself. I was appalled by my appearance. My cheeks seemed drawn, and my eye sockets looked hollow. My eyes were closed, and I studied myself for a bit, because I had never been able to imagine what I would look like with my eyes closed. I looked terrible.

"Just then a nurse came into the room. She must have just come on duty, because I had not seen her before. I had at once an impression of a very conscientious and responsible woman who, though efficient, went about her work with compassion. She took one look at my body, and I perceived a flash of anxiety and concern. She called for orderlies, interns, and other nurses. They all started working over my body, and I thought, 'Oh, no, you don't! I don't want to return to my body. I like it fine up here in a corner of the room!'

"But I began to feel guilty when wave after wave of anxiety began to buffet me from the group of medical personnel who were desperately working to bring me back to life. And I knew I couldn't leave my husband and my kids. I knew that I had better come back.

"Then one of the medics gave my body an injection, and I began to feel drawn back toward my body. It seemed as though there was an opening on the top of my skull. I rolled myself back up and aimed myself like a bullet for that hole.

"Everyone smiled when I opened my eyes, but I knew that I had only come back to pain."

19

An Out-of-Body Walk
With Her Parents in Heaven

Norma Amand of Detroit shared her experience as a living ghost who journeyed to another dimension of existence while under the surgeon's knife in the 1940s:

"My doctor hadn't been honest with me. I knew that I was much sicker than he had told me I was," Norma began her account of her remarkable adventure in the spirit body.

"Two young interns sprinkled the powdered ether onto the face mask while I lay on a wheeled table in the hall outside the operating room. They were talking about what they were going to do on their double-date that night. I thought about how wonderful it was to be young and to be able to plan for the future. I felt that I had come to the end of my life."

Norma next recalled that she suddenly felt as if she were spinning around and around: "I heard a kind of crackling noise, like stiff paper being crunched up into a ball. Then I seemed to be bobbing like a balloon on a string. This is the best comparison that I can make: I was a shining balloon attached to my body by a silver string. I could see my body below me, and the two interns were still chattering about their plans for the evening.

"My doctor came down the hall in a green smock. He took a last puff on a cigarette, then put it in an ashtray filled with white sand.

"He stood beside me, glanced at me, then looked at me carefully and became very angry. He swore at the two interns and scolded them as if they were small boys. He shouted down the hall, and nurses came running. My body was quickly wheeled into the operating room.

"Oh, no, I thought. Something has gone terribly wrong. That's why I'm above everything looking down. I must be dying. I thought of my husband and my two children and I felt sad—not for me, but for them.

"As if from faraway I heard my doctor shouting at the staff, but I didn't really want to watch what was going on in the operating room. I didn't feel any more sickness or pain. I just felt kind of indifferent.

"Then I heard bells tolling, as they do after funerals. Yes, I thought, I must be dead.

"But suddenly a deep voice said, 'Not yet!' And I felt myself being pulled upward and upward, like an arrow being shot into the sky."

The next thing that Norma Armand knew was that she was no longer a shining balloon kind of thing, but she was herself again in the form of her familiar physical body. Standing before her were a number of figures in bright, glowing robes.

"They seemed to glow with an inner radiance. To me, they were what angels are supposed to look like, only they didn't have wings."

"You can stay here for a while," one of the angelic figures told Norma in a gentle voice, "but you will have to go back."

When Norma remembered the experience in her later years, she was certain that she could recall seeing green fields and trees and brooks and streams. "How beautiful Heaven is," she thought. Then, at almost precisely the same time, she reasoned that if she were in Heaven, she should be able to see her parents.

"In a twinkling, Mom and Dad were standing beside me," she said, "and we were all weeping tears of joy at our reunion. Neither of them looked as old as they had when they died, but both of them appeared to be as I remembered them from childhood.

"It seemed as though I visited with them for hours, perhaps even days. Then one of the 'angels' in a white robe came for me and said that it was time for me to return.

"No sooner had he told me this than I was bobbing near the ceiling of a hospital room. I was shocked to hear Father Dupre giving the last rites to my body. My husband was crying, and I had an impression of my younger sister outside in the hall with my children. A nurse stood at the left side of the bed with her fingers on my pulse."

"It is not yet your time," the same deep voice told Norma. She heard that same crackling noise that she had heard before, she saw the color of blood all around her.

"I realized that I was back in my body, and I moaned with the pain of my illness and the just-completed surgery," Norma said. "When I opened my eyes, my husband and Father Dupre were smiling, and the nurse had just returned with our family doctor.

" 'I've been to Heaven,' " I told them.

"Father Dupre chuckled and said that I had them all worried that I might very well be knocking at St. Peter's gate. Our doctor said that he had given me only a matter of a few minutes to pass the crisis or to die. Father Dupre had been called to administer the last rites, because my chances to live seemed almost nonexistent.

"I believe my experience was genuine," Norma concluded her account, "and I told my sister later that I had seen Mom and Dad in Heaven."

20

Encounters With Crisis Apparitions

Whenever a parapsychologist is asked to describe the areas of human experience that present the most favorable climate for psychic phenomena, he will be certain to include the point of death somewhere near the top of his or her list.

Dr. Joseph Rush of Boulder, Colorado, has observed that situations "where the normal, rational sensory-motor system is inadequate or frustrated and blocked for one reason or another" present the type of experience in which ESP functions may come into expression.

Dr. Gardner Murphy commented that death is the most obvious situation which appears to precipitate psychic phenomena, although he includes severe illness and "things that are either biologically or in a broad sense personal crises—disrupting, alerting situations that we have to be ready for, capable of assimilating, warding off, or that call for defense or the ability to incorporate."

Among the most common and universal of all psychic phenomena is that of the "crisis apparition," that ghostly image which is seen, heard, or felt when the individual represented by the spirit form is undergoing a crisis, especially death. It would seem that at the moment of physical death the essential self, the soul, is freed from the confines of the body and is able to soar free of time and space and, in some instances, is able to make a last, fleeting contact with a loved one. These projections at the moment of death betoken that something nonphysical exists within each of us that is capable of making mockery of accepted physical laws—and even more importantly, is capable of surviving physical death.

Betty Mcquire of St. Catherines, Ontario, said that she had been sleeping for a few hours when she was awakened by the form of her brother Sean standing at the foot of the bed. She woke up her husband, but by the time that David had blinked his eyes into wakefulness, the image had disappeared.

"I swear by all the saints that I saw Sean standing right there at the foot of our bed," Betty said with all the passion and conviction she could summon.

David shrugged. "You can see he's not here now. Do you think Sean would break into our house?

It was just a dream. Why are you letting it upset you so?"

Betty could not be swayed. "I saw him as clearly as I see you now. He was standing there wearing a new plaid shirt, one I've never seen him wear before."

David stared at his wife in disbelief, but his obvious doubt did nothing to quiet her.

"It was a green and red plaid, I am certain, though it was hard to make out the colors in the dim light," she went on. "But it had something like leather arrows on the flaps of the two breast pockets."

Betty had scarcely completed the sentence when the telephone rang at their bedside. A policeman grimly informed her that her brother Sean Sullivan had been killed in a motorcycle accident. When she and her husband arrived at the morgue to identify the body, both of them were startled to see the body attired in a plaid shirt such as she had just described.

The crisis apparition is as universal and timeless as death itself, and the pattern is almost exact enough to allow researchers to establish a formula:

The percipient (the one who perceives the phenomena), either preparing for bed or going about some ordinary workaday task, is suddenly and unexpectedly confronted by the image of a loved one. The apparition is clearly identified as that of the beloved, and often gives some sign of parting or affection. Within a very short time after the apparition has faded from view, the percipient receives word that the loved one whose image he has just seen has passed from life to death.

A classic case was recorded as early as 1915 in the *Journal of the American Society for Psychical Research*. Mrs. Margaret Sargent, a certified nurse and the principal percipient, was caring for a young woman at Augusta, Georgia, when, about eleven one evening, the patient took a decided turn for the worse. The doctor did not want to waken the patient's mother, for fear of further upsetting her.

"We knew, however, that the patient ardently desired the presence of her mother," Mrs. Sargent said, "but since she had become unconscious, we did not think it necessary to satisfy that desire."

The doctor and Mrs. Sargent observed the final symptoms setting in, and they stood solemnly by the bedstead awaiting the moment of death. Mrs. Sargent was sitting by the foot of the bed when she looked up to see " . . . a white form advancing, a robed form, although I could not see the face because it was turned in the opposite direction. The form remained for a moment by the inert physical body, then passed swiftly by the doctor and glided toward me, but always turning its face in the opposite direction."

The white-robed form passed through the wall to the room of the sick woman's mother, and as it passed the doctor, it struck him a smart blow on the shoulder.

Startled, the doctor turned around, saw nothing, then said to Mrs. Sargent: "Something hit me on the shoulder."

"It was the woman," she managed-to explain, overcoming her stupefaction. "It was the woman who just passed you."

"What woman?" the doctor asked. "There is no woman in this room but you and that poor dying young lady on the bed. But someone just struck me. What does this mean?"

Before either of them could theorize further about the strange occurrence, the patient began to speak in a feeble voice. To their complete astonishment, the young woman had recovered her senses. She remained completely conscious for another twenty four hours before she died with her head resting lovingly on the arm of her mother.

"It is our absolute conviction," Mrs. Sargent stated, "that, at the time when death was imminent, the soul of the young girl, who idolized her mother, left its own body for the moment to make its last adieux and then returned to its own body again. One must at least admit that a *spirit* was manifested to us that night, that it was visible to me and that it signaled its presence to the doctor by striking him upon the shoulder."

In *The Phenomena of Astral Projection* by Sylvan Muldoon and Hereward Carrington, the authors quote Mrs. Sargent's fascinating account and comment on the blow the doctor received from the spirit by theorizing that such a physical act may have been in vengeance for his refusal to arouse the mother from sleep so that she might be at her dying daughter's bedside. For our purposes, the case offers another powerful example of a situation in which a dying individual found the normal sensory channels of communication blocked, and the intense desire to establish contact with a loved one set in motion a "living ghost."

21

A Child's Beautiful Garden of Love

At the time of her remarkable proof of undying love, Registered Nurse Helen Cosentino was assisting Dr. J. P. Pesek in the pediatrics section of a county hospital. A seven-year-old girl had developed complications following relatively minor surgery, and her fever had shot up during the night. About three o'clock in the morning, the girl seemed to lapse into a comatose state and Nurse Cosentino spent some very anxious moments in the company of the girl's mother and doctor.

Day was just dawning when the girl's fever began to drop and her eyes flickered open. She called for water, and Nurse Cosentino squeezed some water from a soaked cotton ball on her parched lips.

"You gave us a bit of a scare, young lady," Dr. Pesek scolded in mock gruffness. "Are you going to be a good girl now, Wendy, so your mommy can get some sleep?"

Wendy's eyes moved to her mother's drawn features. She frowned and her mouth formed a little "o" of concern. "Mommy, you do look tired," she agreed with Dr. Pesek's diagnosis.

"Never mind," Mrs. Rundle told her daughter, no longer able to hold back the tears of relief. "Mommy is just fine now that her baby is fine."

"You didn't have to worry about me," Wendy told them. "I was playing in the garden with the other boys and girls."

"So you were in the garden, eh?" Dr. Pesek smiled, winking at Nurse Cosentino and Mrs. Rundle. "It must have been a bit cold to play there, wasn't it? December is no time to be playing in a garden."

"Oh, it was nice and sunny," Wendy corrected him. "And all the flowers and bushes were so pretty. The other boys and girls told me that they stay there all the time, but Alisa said that I would have to go back."

"Mommy is so glad that you *did* come back," Mrs. Rundle said, gently pushing aside a lock of her daughter's sweat-soaked hair to kiss her forehead.

Wendy directed her attention to Nurse Cosentino. "Alisa said to tell you that your daddy is all right—and to give your mommy a big kiss from her."

The nurse was stunned. "I could not help feeling a sudden twinge in my inner self when Wendy first mentioned the name Alisa," Helen Cosentino said. "I had a sister named Alisa who died of influenza when she was eight years old. My father had died just three months ago, and he had very much been in my thoughts."

"Please tell me more about Alisa, Wendy," she asked the child, ignoring the frown of Dr. Pesek.

Wendy pursed her lips in thought. "Well, she wore pigtails with yellow ribbons. And her hair was real black."

Alisa had often tied her black pigtails with yellow ribbons.

"There's more that she said," Wendy smiled, crinkling her nose and scrunching her head between her shoulders. "I'll tell you if you give me a real sip of water—and not just drips from that cotton ball."

Nurse Cosentino smiled. "I guess a little sip won't make you sick. If Dr. Pesek says that it is all right."

Dr. Pesek nodded consent, but he wanted to know why the nurse was pursuing an examination of the kind of childish prattle that was so common in a young patient after surgery. "Wendy needs her rest, nurse," he reminded her.

"In a moment," Nurse Cosentino requested as she lowered a drinking glass and straw to Wendy's lips.

After a swallow of water, Wendy kept her part of the bargain. "Alisa said that you should not be afraid to have babies. You shouldn't be afraid that they will die just because she did. She says that it is so beautiful in the garden that she doesn't mind staying there for a while longer. She says that your daddy wants you to have babies, too. You didn't have any while he was around."

"I could barely remain in the child's room," Helen Cosentino said. "But I knew that I had taxed Dr. Pesek's patience and that I had better justify my tiring the girl after her just regaining consciousness.

"Holding back the tears, I told Dr. Pesek and Mrs. Rundle about the death of my only sibling, Alisa, at the age of eight. I explained how my father had died only months before and how he had always complained of not having any grandchildren around. Although I had been married for over nine years, my memories of Alisa's childhood death had been so intense and so terrible, that I had refused to have children.

"I believe with all my being that Wendy somehow traveled to another dimension of reality, a world after physical death, where she met another little girl, my sister Alisa, who had made her transition to that beautiful garden some twenty-three years ago."

22

Receiving Personal Proof of
Life After Death

The idea that we survive physical death, that
some part of our being is immortal, profoundly
affects the lives of those who harbor such a belief.
The orthodox religions promise their congrega-
tions a life eternal, but it cannot be overlooked
that thousands of sincere men and women have
been able to base their hope for a life beyond
the grave on the personal evidence which they
have received from the-visitation of a deceased
loved one.

"It is now the custom in these modern times to
scoff at such accounts of love that has conquered
the grave," one of our interviewees said to us. "I
hope that you will treat these experiences with
the utmost seriousness. Remember, that there

are many, many stricken hearts whose wounds have been healed by the consolation afforded by the conviction that they have, in truth, communicated with the spirits of loved ones who have gone before."

One witness, who *knew* with all his heart that he had seen the surviving spirit of his deceased wife, was terribly hurt when a friend, who prided himself on being a "regular churchgoer," suggested that he had seen an "evil spirit" disguised as his spouse.

"I don't understand why he would say such a thing to me," he said. "Members of every religion believe, hope, or fear that they will survive death. It puzzles me that certain members of orthodox religions say that it is *right* to hope for survival and *wrong* to have it proved to you."

We certainly urge caution in one's accepting too soon that which might be the ministrations of a masquerading entity or deceptive lower dimensional being. But we also know that through the ages hundreds of thousands of people have had the question of whether or not the soul survives physical death answered in the affirmative by their own personal interaction with loved ones who have returned from the sepulchre. For those who have been so blessed, organized religion's hope of a life to come has been transformed from an ethereal promise to a demonstratable guarantee.

On the one hand, our modern materialistic and mechanistic science has done much to obliterate the idea of soul and the duality of mind and body. The concept of mind-soul has been replaced by an emphasis on brain cells, conditioned responses, and memory patterns.

On the other hand, all of the remarkable discoveries in physics in the last few years should make it easier for us to understand and to accept the world of the unseen. The invisible reality of quarks and atoms and moleclues and electrons that form our very existence are now able to be seen because of powerful microscopes and telescopes that can penetrate and examine both the inner space and the outer space that for centuries have been withheld from mortal eyes. The unseen spirit world should no longer require a stretch of imagination or a leap of faith. It simply needs to be better identified and understood.

If you are one who believes in an existence after physical death and who takes the immortality hypothesis seriously, you are probably more concerned with the rather mundane aspects of life after death than you are with the scientific and religio-philosophical implications. You are quite likely more interested in knowing exactly what it is within you that could survive and what kind of world you may expect to await you. Is it possible to be living another existence, walking about in lovely gardens, interacting with other spirits and welcoming those new to the Next World, as in the account of Nurse Helen Cosentino's long-deceased sister Alisa?

To consider these questions in a broad and general sense, we note that theories of survival of the soul range from conceptualizing the seed of man's soul taking root in another physical body via the doctrine of reincarnation, to man assuming an astral body composed of an otherworldly form of matter, to man surmounting death as a disembodied spirit, to man lying in the grave until a spectacular mass day of resurrection. Although we will explore many of these concepts throughout the course of the book, it will probably prove useful to provide an overview of these ideas at this point.

Some of those who claim an interaction with the spirit of a deceased loved one state that they were told that the Next World is a material one composed of some sort of higher matter. Moreover, the world beyond death is a spatial one, having size, shape, and an environment roughly analogous to our own. Perhaps one might more effectively speak of various planes of existence in which the etheric body leaves the physical body at the time of death and advances to another plane, or level, of life. The promised New Jerusalem could then be a substantially real place with a higher concept of geometry and physics than that which we practice on the earth plane.

Some serious thinkers on the subject have expressed their opinion that it is wrong to speak of an afterlife or even of a spirit world. They maintain that there is only one universe and only one life with an infinite number of manifestations and mergers from one gradation to the next. According to this point of view, we are now as much in the spirit world as we will ever be. Death comes when the Essential Self within you withdraws itself from the material world and functions exclusively through your spirit body.

Some of those who have communicated with their deceased loved ones have said that the dead have "awakened" to be greeted by those dear ones who have preceded them. In their understanding, families and friends are reunited in the Next World.

"Those who love us in the larger life have constantly watched over us and usually help when it comes to our own passing," said one who believes in such a spiritual homecoming. "In the Next World, thought is a reality, and they are able to show themselves as they were known on the earth plane."

Although heaven and hell are seldom mentioned in the orthodox theological sense, famed British sensitive Maurice Barbanell, who seemed to be able to demonstrate contact with the world beyond death, once stated that "heaven" and "hell" are real mental states which we have created by the way we have lived our lives. In his view, put forth in such books as *This Is Spiritualism,* spirit life is one of "continuous progress" in which each person gradually eliminates the imperfections in his or her nature and strives toward perfection.

Other theorists have speculated that the soul of the departed will find itself in a world that will be in harmony with its own ideals. "The real hell," suggested one clergyman, "would be to live in a purely carnal world until it becomes a perpetual torment, and the soul realizes its infinite mistakes."

H. H. Price, who once served as president of the Society for Psychical Research, London, put forth the view in Volume 5, Number 1 of *Tomorrow* that the whole point of our life on Earth might be to provide us with a stockpile of memories out of which we might construct an image world at the time of our death. Such a world, Price emphasized, would be a psychic world, not a physical one, even though it might seem a physical world to those experiencing it. The psychic world might, in fact, seem so tangible that the deceased, at first, might find it difficult to realize that he is dead.

The causal laws which these image-objects would obey would not be the laws of physics which control our three-dimensional physical reality, but laws more like those explored by the psychotherapist C. G. Jung. The incoherence of such a dream world of the disembodied would be incoherent only when judged by the nonapplicable laws of conventional physics, for the dream objects would not be physical objects as we would perceive them on the earth plane.

Price theorized that the Next World will be the manifestation in image form of the memories and desires of its occupants, including their repressed or unconscious memories and desires. The soul-created Next World may be every bit as detailed, as vivid, and as complex as is the present three-dimensional world which we now experience.

Price also suggested that the surviving personality may continue to hold a persistent and vivid image of his or her own body. The surviving spirit would be, in actual fact, an immaterial entity; but, Price stated, if it habitually *thinks* of itself as embodied—as it certainly might for a considerable period of time—it would maintain an image of its

earth plane body as the persistent center of the
Next World in the same manner that one's perceived physical body is the persistent nucleus of
one's perceptible reality in the present materially
bound world.

23

A Visit With Grandpa in Another Dimension

In certain instances, men and women who have survived near-death experiences have reported encountering spirits of the dead in what appeared to them to be a material environment that existed somewhere in another dimension.

In the fall of 1987, Carl Velders, a thirty-three-year-old mountain bike enthusiast, went into a bad slide on a trail outside of Salida, Colorado, and was knocked unconscious.

"I seemed to be spinning like a crazy top," he remembered, "and then this old guy seemed to reach out and slow me down."

Carl felt that he must be dead, and the old man had to be Death himself.

The man smiled at him and squeezed his arm in a fatherly way. "I'm not Death. You won't meet him for a while yet. Come and sit a while."

His host indicated a small, neat house with a front porch that offered both a swing and a comfortable looking rocking chair. Carl knew that he had seen that house somewhere, some time long ago.

He looked more closely at the old man. "There was something familiar about him. The white mustache, the thinning hair, the plaid flannel shirt. I had a flash of some old pictures in one of the family albums. Then I saw Peaches, Grandpa Angstrom's old ginger-haired mutt, and I knew that the old man was my grandfather who had died when I was around three."

Carl identifed the elderly gentleman as his grandfather Angstrom, and received a warm smile and a strong embrace in response. "Are you sure that I'm not dead, Grandpa?" Carl had to ask.

Grandfather Angstrom told him that he had just received a very nasty blow to the head. He said that it was possible for the spirit to leave the physical body and then go back to it.

"He told me to look down, and I could see my body—I mean my physical body—all smashed up at the side of the trail. A car came along, and some guys stopped and got out to look at me. One of them knelt and turned me over. I yelled at him to be careful: 'Don't you know that you aren't supposed to move the body of an accident victim? You could be grinding my broken bones or driving splinters into my organs!' "

Grandpa Angstrom laughed and assured him that nothing was broken. "You inherited my thick Swedish skull, by golly! You're just going to have a really bad headache for many days."

"There were so many questions that I wanted to ask my grandfather," Carl said wistfully. "I was just about to ask him more about the process of death and dying when I saw one of the guys beside my body on the mountain trail pull a flask from his pocket and shove it between my lips. The next thing I knew I was choking and sputtering on some cheap Scotch.

"I don't know how many members of our family really believed that I had seen Grandpa Angstrom," Carl admitted, "but I really don't care. I know that I have received my personal proof of survival and the eternal bonds of family love. I have also lost my formerly morbid fear of death."

24

Her Husband's Spirit Returned to Pay the Mortgage

In the March 1957 issue of *Fate* magazine, Mrs. Minnie Harris told how her dead husband returned to pay the mortgage.

It was during the hard Depression year of 1932 that John Harris had his skull crushed by the wildly kicking hooves of their mule. John had just returned from town with ten crisp new one-hundred dollar bills which he had withdrawn from the bank in order to pay off their loan to a money-lender they had nicknamed "Old Skinflint."

In the sudden tragedy of her husband's death, Minnie had forgotten all about the money until the undertaker had come to remove John's body. When she searched his clothing, she was shocked to discover that the envelope containing the ten bills was missing.

Minnie's mother arrived, and the two women went over John's clothing inch by inch and searched the house, the closets, the cupboards, even the feed bins in the barn. Minnie trusted the neighbor who had helped her with John's body. She knew that their friend Bill would not have stolen the money.

Only one explanation remained: John had hidden the money just before he was killed by the terrible hooves of the mule. "Old Skinflint's" note would be due in a couple of weeks, and he would foreclose and take the Harris home without the slightest hesitation unless the money was forthcoming.

A week before the note was due, Minnie received a curt, unsympathetic reminder from the money lender that he most certainly did expect the money on the appointed date, regardless of the unexpected death in the Harris family.

In renewed desperation, Minnie searched under sacks of mash, beneath the straw in the hens' nest, in tool chests; but she could not find the one thousand dollars that would keep the money-lender from foreclosing on the farm.

Three days before the note was due, Minnie had a dream in which John came to her and tried to tell her where he had hidden the money. "But he couldn't speak because of his broken jaw," Minnie remembered her anguish. "I screamed at him as he turned sadly to leave the room. I begged him to come back and to tell me where he had put the money."

But in spite of her desperate cries, John melted into mist; and Minnie came awake in cold perspiration to find her mother trying to shake her awake. Minnie was half-resentful that her mother had awakened her. She was convinced that the spirit of her dead husband would have given her some clue to the whereabouts of the money if she had been allowed to continue her dream.

The next night she sat up in bed late, reading her Bible, searching out all the verses which dealt with dreams and visions. When at last she fell into a fitful sleep, she saw John appear in the doorway and motion to her to follow him. Minnie screamed at him to wait for her—then she was abruptly awakened once again by her mother.

On the third night Minnie went to bed with the conviction that John would once again return and attempt to communicate with her. She begged her mother not to awaken her no matter how loudly she might scream.

It was nearly dawn when the image of John appeared at her bedside, took her hand and led her to the kitchen door. Minnie saw that it had snowed during the night and the rising sun was painting a rosy glow over the barnyard and fields. John pointed to his footprints leading from the door to the big haystack at the corner of the barn. Then he was transformed into a fleecy cloud and melted away like vapor before the sun.

Minnie found herself back in bed, the morning sun shining across her face. She threw on a robe, ran to the kitchen door. The newly fallen snow was smooth and unmarked, but in her memory of the dream-vision, she could still see her husband's footprints zigzagging through the snow.

She paused only to slip on a coat and a pair of overshoes. She found the money in a tobacco tin which had been hidden deep under the hay.

25

Wally Knocked at the Door But He Couldn't Come In

Tammy Swensen said that her mother, Esther, had been terribly lonely for nine years after her father died. "I was so pleased when, after 'keeping company' for three years, Mom married Wally Johnson, a widower who had also suffered much heartbreak in the six years since his wife and three daughters were killed in an airplane crash."

Tammy clearly remembers the night when the remarkable manifestation of spirit occurred. "I was seventeen, still living at home with Mom and Wally. Mom was about forty then. I think Wally was three or four years older. They had been married for less than a year, but they had some really happy times. I think they might even have discussed having a baby together."

On this particular night, Wally had been called to another state because of his business. Tammy was getting ready for a date when both she and her mother heard a knock at the door.

"Since I had not finished putting on my makeup, I asked Mom to answer the door," Tammy said. "I was a bit ticked off at my date for coming so early, but Mom smiled at me and told me to be happy that the guy didn't come late and sit in the car and honk for me."

Tammy sat before her bedroom mirror, hastily applying eye shadow. She heard her mother open the door, and she could hear her speaking, but she couldn't understand what she was saying.

"I couldn't figure out why she didn't ask my date to come in. I got kind of upset, thinking maybe he was telling her that he couldn't go out that night. But that was crazy. Why would he have come over to tell me the bad news when he could have telephoned?"

In a few moments, her mother entered Tammy's bedroom. She looked pale, and she was chewing at a corner of her lower lip in the way that she did when she was nervous. "That was Wally," she said in a puzzled tone.

"Wally!" Tammy echoed her surprise and confusion. "What's he doing home? And where is he?"

Tammy and her mother both knew that Wally had been gone for about a week, and they did not expect him to return home for at least another five or six days.

"When I asked him to come into the apartment,"

her mother said slowly, as if she were cautiously considering her words, "he just stood there. He shook his head sadly, looking as if he were about to cry. Then he turned and walked away from me."

Tammy ran to the front door of their apartment and opened it. Wally Johnson was nowhere to be seen.

She ran quickly down the stairs. There was no car in front of the apartment house, and she could see no men walking on the street. Wally could not have disappeared from sight in the brief time that had passed since Tammy and her mother had heard the knock on the door and the few seconds in which Esther Johnson had described his appearance at their door.

"Just as I was about to return to our apartment," Tammy said, "my date arrived. I asked him if he minded if we stayed with my mother for just a few minutes before we left. I could guess what was going through Mom's mind, and I didn't want her to be alone just then.

"But by the time that we entered the apartment, Mom was on the telephone. When she hung up, she nearly became hysterical. Wally's business partner had called to inform her that Wally had been stricken with a heart attack and had died at the very moment that his ghost knocked on our door."

Although Tammy did not see the image of Wally Johnson, she had been very much aware that her mother was carrying on a conversation with someone who refused to enter the apartment.

"In my teenaged anxiety, I assumed that it was my date with an excuse not to go out that night and refusing to enter the apartment to face me," Tammy recalled. "Instead, it was the ghost of a sorrowful husband who had come to inform his new wife that their time together was to be a tragically short one. I will never forget this experience—or the sound of that knock on our door!"

26

His Mother's Spirit Gave Him Good Advice— Whether He Wanted to Listen or Not!

Barry Cassidy did his best to shut himself off from the uncomfortable feelings of humiliation that depressed him when he considered that, at the age of 36, he was once again living in his parents' home while he was in the process of obtaining a divorce so that he might marry the "other woman."

"My marriage had turned out to be a miserable facade that had crumbled around both my wife's and my ears," Barry said. "Jody and I had married right out of college, two 'yuppies' determined to get rich as fast as morally possible. I can't blame Jody for staying on the super-fast materialistic treadmill because her rewards were incredible. On the other hand, my more traditional rearing had forced me to see how shallow we were both becoming, and I insisted on taking more time to smell the roses and enjoy life."

It was on one of those occasions when he was "smelling the roses" during a walk in the park that Barry had met Morena, a woman who seemed more sympathetic to a balanced lifestyle.

"Our affair didn't shoot off with a fireworks display of passion," Barry explained. "I discovered that she jogged nearly every night in that park, and I made it a point to be there. After a few weeks, I was jogging with her back to her apartment overlooking the river."

It was during the second month that he had been living with his parents that Barry's mother suffered a massive stroke.

"I hoped that my personal problems had not prompted Mom's stroke," Barry recalled. "Dad assurred me that their doctor had tried to warn her to take it easier and that it was, sadly, perhaps in the order of natural events.

"I was coming home from seeing Morena at about 1:30 in the morning when I saw nearly every light in the house shining out at me. Because Mom had been in intensive care for four days, I got a really queasy feeling in the pit of my stomach."

Barry found his father Dick Cassidy and his sister Lori sitting at the dining room table silently sipping coffee.

"As soon as they looked up at me, I knew that Mom was dead. Lori's eyes were swollen from crying, and Dad looked pale and drawn. He looked far older than his 62 years when he told me that

Mom had died of a massive coronary just a few hours before."

Lori left for her apartment around 2:30, and Barry's father went into his bedroom to lie down and attempt to get some rest.

"I decided to sit in the old recliner in the living room before going to bed. Because of the light coming from the chandelier in the dining room, I could have read if I had wished, but I chose to lean back and permit the memories of Mom to come forth unchecked.

"I remembered how frightened I was to leave her side and to start my first day at school. I would never forget the kind manner in which she comforted me when my 'best friend,' Grandpa Mortensen had died. My memory banks flooded my brain with rapidly fleeting images of bruised knees, teeth under my pillow for the Tooth Fairy, the best oatmeal cookies in the world, and then I thought of the dream that she had related just a few weeks after I had moved back home."

Lorna Cassidy had told him that she had dreamed of her own death. "Buddy," she had begun, calling him by her pet name for him, "I saw myself walking toward beautiful green rolling meadows with the loveliest flowers imaginable. I was wearing a white, flowing robe, and I was following a path that I knew would lead me to heaven."

Barry felt the tears coming as he spoke aloud to the empty room, "Oh, Mom, did you know that you were going to die? Did you know that your time to move on to a higher dimension was almost upon you?"

"*Yes!*"

The voice that answered Barry made his spine go rigid. Startled, his eyes searched the room for whomever had answered his unspoken question.

"It was a woman's voice," Barry remembered, "that I knew for certain. And I also knew that the voice sounded just exactly like my mother's."

Barry nervously decided that he had fallen asleep in the comfortable recliner and had dreamed of his mother. It was time, he argued convincingly, to go to bed and try to fall back to sleep.

"That's when I saw Mom. She appeared as a transparent figure, glowing with a soft, white light. She said that she had come back to warn me, but first she wanted to tell me that she had been walking on those same green, rolling meadows that she had seen in her dream."

She went on to say that where she was now, there was no pain or hatred, only peace and contentment.

"And if *you* want some peace and contentment in your earthlife," she warned Barry. "You had better listen to what I have to say.

"Morena is not the kind of woman that you now believe her to be," Lorna Cassidy continued. "If you go ahead with the divorce from Jody and marry Morena, you will be sorry. Your future will not be at all as you now imagine it. You believe that Morena is giving you another chance at happiness. I tell you, my son, that you are, instead, taking a chance with your immortal soul! If you should not heed my advice, Barry, and if you should marry Morena, she will divorce you within three years of your marriage. And she will be merciless in the settlement!"

Barry said that his mother's spirit form stayed with him for about five minutes. "I kept pinching myself and touching my eyes to be certain that I was awake and not dreaming. Then, because I was so very much in love with Morena, I began to question Mom about the validity of her warning. Surely, she must be mistaken."

The spirit form remained adamant. "My son, that woman is not as you believe her to be. She will hurt you terribly if you marry her."

To his everlasting regret, Barry managed to convince himself that the spirit visitation of his mother had only been a troubled dream brought about by grief and emotional stress.

"If only I hadn't been such a rationalist, such a materialist," Barry vainly protested his past decision. "If only I hadn't believed myself to be so much in love with Morena. Mom's advice from the spirit world proved to be totally accurate. Morena brought me to new depths of despair when we divorced after three years of a miserable marriage."

27

His Best Friend Returned to Prove the Soul Survives Death

Dan Fowler's cousin Pete was not only his kin, but he was also his best friend.

"We were always together," Dan stated in his account of Pete's manifestation of undying love. "We lived about three blocks apart, just the right distance to warm up on our bikes for an excursion around the middle-sized Nebraska town which our family had called home for three generations."

One Sunday evening after the boys had taken in a matinee at the larger of the town's two motion picture theaters, Dan found himself extremely depressed.

"We had gone to a movie that we both thought was an action-adventure picture, but which turned out to be a real five-hankie weeper. At the end, a young boy, about our age, in his early teens, dies in the arms of his weeping mother. The scene had shaken me to the very core of my youthful existence, for I had a great fear of death and dying."

"Hey, Danny, be cool," Pete tried to comfort him as they sat around the kitchen table and spooned into the generous bowls of chocolate swirl ice cream that his mother had set before them. "Dying isn't such a bad thing, you know."

Dan wanted to know the source of Pete's cheerful insight.

"I know that when we die we are all going to go to a better place."

"Oh, yeah?" Dan questioned.

"Heaven is going to be wonderful," Pete went on. "It's going to be . . . well, it's going to be . . . heavenly, that's what."

Dan recalled that Pete's face would almost become illuminated as he spoke of heaven and the afterlife.

"I don't know where Pete received his special knowledge of heaven," Dan said. "Neither of our families were very faithful churchgoers. I don't think that Pete had even been to Sunday School."

Once when the two boys were camping out down by the creek, Dan set forth his argument that once you quit breathing and your heart stops, you are dead—stone-cold dead and that's it. "Then you're nothing but a meal ticket for the worms!"

Pete laughed at his cousin's dour pessimism. "You old sour puss. I'll tell you what. When I die, I'll come back and say a special good-bye to you."

Dan couldn't stand such turns in the conversation. He couldn't imagine life without his best friend and first cousin. "Stop that, Pete! Don't talk about dying. Let's just not talk about it anymore, okay?"

"Scaredy-cat Danny," Pete teased. Then he became very serious. "Here's one thing more. When I die, I'll come back and give you a special farewell right in the old Ford Hotel."

Not counting the three or four motels on the edge of town, the Ford Hotel was the only classic hotel that their Nebraska hometown could support. The place had a lot of history connected with it. It was built back in the 1880s, and some people said that Buffalo Bill and Annie Oakley had stayed there once. Pete loved the place, especially the elevators, and the two boys used to spend hours there, guessing the life stories of the people who checked in.

"I'm sure, Pete," Dan laughed at his cousin's prediction. "I'm sure that your ghost is going to haunt the elevators in the Ford Hotel!"

Then both the boys laughed at Pete as a spook scaring the hotel guests.

Danny was eleven. Pete was twelve and a half. On that summer night by the creek, they both knew that they would each live at least a hundred more years. They counted shooting stars until they fell asleep.

Two months later, just a few days after school had resumed in September, Pete was struck by a feed truck from the farmers' elevator. He had been riding his bike en route to little league baseball practice. An elderly woman stepped down from her front steps directly into his path, and he swerved out into the street to avoid hitting her. The truck threw Pete for thirty feet or more. He died on the way to the hospital in Lincoln. His bicycle was crumpled and twisted like a discarded gum wrapper.

Somehow, Dan managed to get through the funeral. His memories of the next several days are completely befogged.

"I would wake up in the morning and start to call Pete to see where we would meet for lunch that day after noon class ended. Then I would remember that he was dead, and the sorrow would hit me again like an avalanche of grief. I dreamed at night that Pete was still alive, but he was hiding out, playing a joke on everyone but me, his best friend and confidante."

A few months after Pete's funeral, George Cook, Dan's uncle, asked him to lunch at the Ford Hotel's dining room. "I was really excited," Dan remembered. "I had never eaten in the Ford before, and I felt really adult. Also, I felt that I would somehow be close to Pete there, since he loved the old place so much."

During lunch, Uncle George asked Dan how he was doing without Pete around. Everyone knew that the two boys had been inseparable, and that Dan had taken his cousin's death very hard.

"Uncle George had once studied to be a preacher before he went back to farming, so I figured that the family had nominated him to provide me with some counseling. That was all right. I liked Uncle George. He always smelled of sen-sen and Wildroot cream oil."

Dan told his uncle that Pete had once promised to return to the very hotel in which they were sitting and to haunt him there. Dan started to cry a little, and he felt embarrassed, unmanly, even though he knew Uncle George was a kind and understanding man.

"Well, now, Danny," Uncle George said in his soft manner of speaking. "I don't know if I rightly believe in haunts and ghosts and stuff like that, but we know that Jesus Christ promised us that we would see our loved ones again if we kept on that straight and narrow pathway to heaven."

Dan had no wish to enter a theological debate with Uncle George, who probably counted as half a preacher. "I hope that is true, Uncle George. I surely do."

"Be of faith, boy," Uncle George promised. "It is true."

After lunch, Uncle George excused himself to head for what he always referred to as "the little boys' room," and Dan walked slowly out into the lobby, his mind flooded with a hundred memories of the times that he had staked out the Ford Hotel with Pete.

"As I walked down the hall, I saw the elevator doors slide open for a boy about my age who was waiting to get inside. The kid stepped in, then turned to face me. *It was Pete!*

"He grinned at me, winked, then waved that kind of strange salute he always gave me when we said good-bye to each other. Then the doors closed.

"I started bawling right there in front of the elevators, and I didn't care who saw me or if they thought I was the biggest baby in Nebraska. Pete had come back to haunt me in the Ford Hotel, just as he had promised. He came back to say goodbye and to prove to me that life is eternal."

28

Classic Cases of Love
That Reached Beyond the Grave

William E. Sorensen discovered the following account written on yellowed sheets in an old family Bible that belonged to a cousin who lived in Holstebro in Jutland, Denmark. The tale, which Sorenson first related in the July, 1959, issue of *Fate* magazine, tells of an apparition of a dying man that appeared to his sweetheart and five witnesses.

Eighteen-year-old Dora Starcke, who later became Dora Sorensen, the grandmother of William and his cousin, was engaged to marry Arne Borglum, a cavalryman who was among the first men to be called in 1864 when Denmark was attacked by Germany and Austria. Dora and Arne planned to be married as soon as he could arrange a long furlough; but in the meantime, the young warrior had no choice other than to be with his troop at the border.

Shortly after 8:00 P.M. on April 18, 1864, Dora, her parents, her two brothers, and her sister were seated in the parlor of the farmhouse, occupied with reading, knitting, and casual discussions of planting time.

Suddenly, they all saw Arne standing just inside the door leading to a hall. He looked exactly as when they had last seen him, except that he was pale, his blue uniform was splotched with mud, and his saber was missing—the scabbard at his side hung empty. Dora's father particularly noted the empty scabbard, for he had been a cavalryman himself.

The entire family sat in complete bewilderment before the image of Arne Borglum. The last any of them had heard, he was stationed at the front.

Slowly, Dora rose and started toward Arne to welcome him. She could only imagine one thing. He had been granted the long furlough for their wedding.

As the rest of her family got to their feet to shake Arne's hand and to bid him welcome, Dora quickened her pace to embrace her fiance. She was within but a few feet of Arne when he vanished forever from her sight.

Since the apparition had been so clearly seen by all six members of the Starcke family, their reaction was one of consternation and grief. According to Sorenson, the Starckes held no doubt regarding the ominous significance of the vision.

About a week later, a letter from one of Borglum's comrades told how Arne had died in fierce combat on a road near Flensburg. He had single-handedly fought off five Austrian hussars, but one of them managed at last to shoot him in the back and to wrest the saber from his dying hand. Arne had died at the precise time that his apparition had appeared in the Starcke farmhouse. The image of Arne Borglum had manifested itself to his fiancee and her family exactly as he had appeared at the moment of his death, even to the empty scabbard at his side.

THE PARANORMAL EXPERIENCES OF CHARLES DICKENS

The British novelist Charles Dickens, who, in addition to the classic stories *A Tale of Two Cities* and *Oliver Twist*, brought the world his famous ghosts of Christmases Past, Present, and Future, as well as the spirit of old Marley with his clanking chains, testified in his own words that he had experienced some personal encounters with the etheric realms. Dickens wrote how he awakened one morning to see the apparition of his father sitting by his bed: "As he did not move, I became alarmed and laid my hand upon his shoulder . . . and there was no such thing."

Dickens' most remarkable paranormal experience came to him after the death of his young, beloved sister-in-law Mary Hogarth in 1837. Dickens was terribly bereaved over Mary's sudden, tragic passing, and shortly after the girl's death,

Dickens began experiencing nocturnal visitations from Mary's spirit, as the attractive apparition regularly invaded his dreams. The lovely spirit became, in Dickens' own words, " . . . as inseparable from my existence as the beating of my heart is."

The entity stepped out of Dickens' dreams on at least one occasion. The novelist testified that he could not clearly see the face of the phantom that appeared before him on one occasion, but he was convinced that it was his Mary.

"I was not at all afraid," he wrote, "but in a great delight, so that I wept very much, and stretching out my arm to it, called it 'Dear.' I entreated it, as it rose above my bed and soared up to the vaulted roof . . . to answer a question . . . touching the future life. My hands were still outstretched towards it as it vanished."

As we have stated, documented stories of such apparitions may be found in the literature of all eras and all cultures. Images of loved ones who have come to say farewell, to demonstrate survival after physical death, to provide valuable information previously unknown, and to offer comfort and solace to their beloved before their transition to a higher plane of existence, appear to rich and poor, famous and obscure alike.

The skeptic's question of whether or not such images of the deceased loved ones are truly proof of their continued existence after the grave has no relevancy to those men and women who have been blessed with the appearance of a dear mate, a sweetheart, a child, a parent, or a friend after the moment of their physical death.

In this chapter we will present a number of remarkable cases suggestive of survival after death from the annals of psychical research. These cases have become classics because in each instance the apparitions of the loved ones left the witness with some bit of veridical information, that is, information which was previously unknown to the witness and which could be later verified.

THE SCRATCH ON THE CHEEK

In 1876, Mr. F. G., a traveling salesman, was sitting in a hotel room in St. Joseph, Missouri. It was high noon, and he was smoking a cigar and writing out orders.

Suddenly conscious of someone sitting on his left with one arm resting on the table, the salesman was startled to look up into the face of his dead sister, a young lady of eighteen who had died of cholera in 1867.

"So sure was I that it was she," he wrote later in an account to the American Society for Psychical Research (Proceedings, S.P.R., VI, 17), "that I sprang forward in delight, calling her by name."

As he did so, the image of his sister vanished. The salesman resumed his seat, stunned by the experience. The cigar was still in his mouth, the pen was still in his hand, the ink was still moist on the order blank. He was completely satisfied that he was wide awake and had not been dreaming.

"I was near enough to touch her, had it been a physical possiblity, and noted her features, expression, and details of dress . . . She appeared as if alive. Her eyes looked kindly and perfectly naturally into mine. Her skin was so lifelike that I could see the glow or moisture on its surface . . ."

On the whole, Mr. F. G. noted, there was no change in his sister's appearance, but he was intrigued by what seemed to be a bright red line or a scratch on the right side of her face.

He was so impressed by the experience that he took the next train home to tell his parents about the remarkable visitation. His mother nearly fainted when Mr. F. G. mentioned the bright red line or the scratch on his sister's face.

With tears streaming down her cheeks, she told him that he had indeed seen his sister, for only she was aware of that scratch that she had accidentally made while doing some little act of kindness after her daughter's death. His mother said that she had carefully obliterated all traces of the slight scratch with the aid of powder.

"And this she had never mentioned to a human being from that day to this," F. G. stated.

It seems far more than coincidence when F. G., the narrator, adds: "A few weeks later my mother died, happy in her belief that she would rejoin her favorite daughter in a better world."

In commenting upon this classic case, the noted psychic researcher Frederick W. H. Myers, wrote that, in his opinion, the spirit of the daughter had perceived the approaching death of her mother and had appeared to the brother in order to force him into the role of message bearer. Also, by prompting F. G. to return home unexpectedly at that time, the spirit of his sister enabled him to have a final visit with their mother.

Myers is further intrigued by the fact that the spirit entity appeared not as a corpse, but as a girl full of health and happiness, " . . . with the symbolic red mark worn simply as a test of identity."

RAYMOND'S LAST PHOTOGRAPH

The son of the noted British physicist, Sir Oliver Lodge, was killed on September 14, 1915 in his capacity as a medical officer of the Second South Lancers. On September 27, Lady Lodge sat with a medium who described a photograph that had been taken of Raymond with a group of fellow officers. Lady Lodge said that she knew of no such photograph.

"Your son is very particular that I should tell you of this photograph," the medium insisted. "In one photograph, you see his walking stick."

The Lodges had numerous photographs of their son, but they did not possess a single one depicting a group of medical officers in which Raymond would be included. Sir Oliver, however, was impressed with the emphasis that the medium had placed upon their son, being insistent that they should be told of this photograph.

Then, according to Sir Oliver's report on the case (Proceedings, S.P.R. Vol. XXIX), on November 29, they received a letter from a Mrs. Cheves, who was a stranger to them, but who was the mother of a friend of Raymond's. By marvelous coincidence, she informed them that she had half-a-dozen photographs of a sitting by a group of medical officers in which Raymond and her son were present. Would the Lodges, Mrs. Cheves inquired, like to have a copy of the photograph?

Sir Oliver and his wife responded immediately in the affirmative, and in the interim before the photograph arrived, Lady Lodge went through Raymond's diary and found an entry dated August 24 which told of such a photo having been taken.

Sir Oliver noted in his report that since the exposure had been made only twenty-one days before his death, Raymond may never have seen a print of the sitting. "He certainly never mentioned it in his letters," Sir Oliver stated. "We were therefore in complete ignorance of it."

While the Lodges were awaiting a copy of the photograph from Mrs. Cheves, they visited another medium through whose control the spirit of their son provided them with additional details concerning the group picture. There were a dozen or more people in the photograph, Raymond said. He named two friends who were prominently featured and said that he himself was sitting down with officers behind him, one of whom annoyed him by leaning on his shoulder.

When the photograph was delivered to the Lodge home on the afternoon of December 7, Sir Oliver and Lady Lodge noted at once that the picture offered a poor likeness of Raymond, but excellent evidence that their son had communicated to them from beyond the grave. The walking stick was there, though not under Raymond's arm, as the first medium had said. The fellow officers Raymond had named through the second medium, were in the photograph, and the general arrangement of the men was as the mediums described it.

"But by far the most striking piece of evidence is the fact that someone sitting behind Raymond is leaning or resting a hand on his shoulder," commented Sir Oliver. "The photograph fortunately shows the actual occurence, and . . . indicates that Raymond was rather annoyed with it; for his face is a little screwed up, and his head has been slightly bent to one side out of the way of the man's arm. It is the only case in the photograph where one man is leaning or resting his hand on the shoulder of another."

In his *My Philosophy* (London, 1933), Sir Oliver Lodge wrote: "I am absolutely convinced not only of survival, but of demonstrated survival, demonstrated by an occasional interaction with matter in such a way as to produce physical results."

THE WILL OF JAMES CHAFFIN

On September 7, 1921, James Chaffin of Davie County, North Carolina, died as the result of a fall. A farmer, Chaffin was survived by his widow and four sons, but the will which he had had duly attested by two witnesses on November 16, 1905, left all of his property to the third son, Marshall.

One night in the latter part of June, 1925, four years after James Chaffin's death, James Pinkney

Chaffin, the farmer's second son, saw the spirit figure of the deceased standing at his bedside and heard the specter tell of another will. According to the son, Chaffin had appeared dressed as he often had in life.

"You will find the will in my overcoat pocket," the spirit figure said, taking hold of the garment and pulling it back.

The next morning, the son arose convinced that he had seen and heard his father and that the spirit had visited him for the purpose of correcting some error. His father's black overcoat had been passed on to John Chaffin, so James traveled to Yadkin County to examine the pocket to which the spirit had made reference.

The two brothers found that the lining of the inside pocket had been sewn together, and when they cut the stitches, they found a roll of paper which bore the message: "Read the 27th chapter of Genesis in my daddies old Bible."

James Pinkney Chaffin was then convinced that the apparition had spoken truthfully, and he brought witnesses with him to the home of his mother where, after some search, they located the dilapidated old Bible in the top drawer of a dresser in an upstairs room. One of the witnesses found the will in a pocket which had been formed by folding two of the Bible's pages together.

The new will had been made by James Chaffin on January 16, 1919, fourteen years after the first will. In this testament, the farmer stated that he desired his property to be divided equally among his four sons with the admonition that they provide for their mother as long as she lived.

Although the second will had not been attested, it would, under North Carolina law, be considered valid because it had been written completely in James Chaffin's own handwriting. All that remained was to present sufficient evidence that the hand that had written the second will was, without doubt, that of the deceased.

Marshall Chaffin, the sole beneficiary under the conditions of the old will, had passed away within a year of his father, nearly four years before the spirit of James Chaffin had appeared to his second son, James Pinkney Chaffin. Marshall's widow and son prepared to contest the validity of the second will, but those who predicted a long and bitter legal battle were disappointed when ten witnesses arrived in the courtroom prepared to give evidence that the second will was truly in James Chaffin's handwriting.

After they saw the will, Mrs. Marshall Chaffin and her son immediately withdrew their opposition. It seemed evident that they, too, believed the will had been written in the hand of the testator.

James Pinkney later told an investigator for the *Journal of the Society for Psychical Research* that his father had appeared to him before the trial and told him that the lawsuit would be terminated in such a manner.

"Many of my friends do not believe it is possible for the living to hold communication with the dead," James Pinkey said, "but I am convinced that my father actually appeared to me on these several occasions; and I shall believe it to the day of my death."

It does seem strange that James Chaffin kept

secret the existence of the second will, especially in view of the fact that his disturbed spirit came back from beyond the grave to right the wrong that had been done to his widow and three disinherited sons. Perhaps the farmer had intended some sort of deathbed revelation and these plans were left unrealized when his life was cut short by accident.

GRANDAD HAS JUST DIED

On the night of June 11, 1923, Mrs. Gladys Watson had been asleep for three or four hours when she was awakened by someone calling her name. As she sat up in bed, she was able to discern the form of her beloved grandfather leaning toward her.

"Don't be frightened, it's only me. I have just died," the image told her.

Mrs. Watson started to cry and reached across the bed to awaken her husband.

"This is how they will bury me," Grandad Parker said, indicating his suit and black bow tie. "Just wanted to tell you I've been waiting to go ever since Mother was taken."

The Watson's house was next door to the Lilly Laboratories in Indianapolis. The bedroom was dimly illuminated with lights from the laboratory. Grandad Parker was clearly and solidly to be seen. Then, before Gladys could awaken her husband, Grandad Parker had disappeared.

Mr. Watson insisted that she had had a nightmare. "Your grandfather is alive and well back in Wilmington," he told her.

Gladys Watson was certain that it was not a dream. She knew that she had seen Grandad Parker and that he had come to bid her farewell.

It was 4:05 A.M. when Watson called Gladys' parents in Wilmington to prove to his distraught wife that Grandad Parker's appearance in their bedroom had only been a nightmare.

His mother-in-law was surprised to receive the call. She had been up most of the night with Grandad, her father-in-law, and had been waiting for morning before she would let the Watsons know that Gladys' grandfather had passed away at 4:00 A.M.

Mrs. Watson had been awakened by the fully externalized apparition of her grandfather at approximately 3:30 A.M., Indianapolis time. Her husband had got out of bed and made the telephone call at about 4:05 A.M. Grandad Parker had died at 4:00 A.M. Eastern Time—half an hour before Gladys Watson received her final visit from her grandfather.

Mrs. Watson wrote an account of her experience for the *Journal of the American Society for Psychical Research* (Vol. LXV, No. 3) in which she mentioned that both she and her husband were children of Methodist ministers " . . . schooled against superstition from the time of their birth."

Gladys Watson described the experience as if Grandad Parker had been there in the flesh, speaking in a " . . . soft, yet determined voice."

Rev. Walter E. Parker, Sr., Mrs. Watson's father, corroborated her story in a letter to the A.S.P.R.: "Gladys had always been my father's favorite grandchild, and we had promised to let her know if and when he became seriously ill. (He made his home with us) He took sick the day before. We called the doctor and thought he was going to be all right. The end came suddenly around four o'clock in the morning. We were going to wait until later in the morning to get in touch with Gladys. I believe sincerely in the truth of this experience as my daughter writes it."

A MESSAGE TO MOTHER

On February 10, 1933, the trumpet in the darkened seance room of the famous spirit medium Estelle Roberts moved toward Maurice Barbanell, and the voice of a young girl began to speak in a hesitant manner.

"Come along," he encouraged the disembodied voice. "Come and talk to me."

"I am Bessy Manning, and I want you to send a message to my mother," the voice told the editor of *Psychic News*. "Mother has been reading some of your articles about direct-voice seances. Please tell her you spoke to me."

Barbanell assured the spirit voice that he would send whatever message that she relayed.

"Tell Mother I still have my long plaits," the voice began. "I am twenty-two and have blue eyes. I died with tuberculosis last Easter. I have brought my brother who was killed by a motor car. Could you bring Mother here?"

Although Barbanell was sympathetic to the request that was put to him, he needed more essential information if he were to fulfill his promise to the spirit. "I must know where your mother lives," he said simply enough.

The reply came without hesitation: "14 Canterbury Street, Blackburn."

The next day Maurice Barbanell sent a telegram to Bessy Manning's mother telling her that "Red Cloud," Estelle Roberts' spirit control, had brought her daughter through during a seance the night before. The address which the spirit had given him proved to be correct, and within a few days, Barbanell received a reply. The letter from the Mannings told of their "glorious happiness" at the contact which Red Cloud's spirit circle had achieved with Bessy.

Mrs. Manning substantiated the information which the spirit had given Barbanell during the direct-voice seance. Bessy had passed on the preceding Easter, and her brother had been killed in an automobile accident nine years before.

In his book *This Is Spiritualism*, Barbanell stated that he regarded Bessy Manning's return as "flawless evidence for the afterlife." In his opinion, no theories of telepathy or the subconscious mind could explain away the truth of this dramatic case of spirit contact. He also dismissed any suggestion of collusion or any other kind of fraud: "Mrs. Manning had never met Estelle Roberts, or corresponded with her or any member of her family. Neither had she written to me or anyone who attended those voice seances. Yet her daughter's full name and address had been given, accompanied by a complete message which was accurate in every detail."

Barbanell later arranged for Mrs. Manning to travel to London so that she might speak to the voice of Bessy and judge for herself whether or not her daughter had survived the grave.

After the seance, Mrs. Manning wrote to Maurice Barbanell that she had heard her own daughter speak to her "in the same old loving way . . . with the same peculiarities of speech." Mrs. Manning went on to declare that the spirit of Bessy had spoken of incidents that she was certain no other person could know. "I, her mother, am the best judge, and I swear before Almighty God it was Bessy. . . . I have no fear of so-called death. I am looking forward to the glorious meeting with my loved ones."

BISHOP PIKE CONTACTS HIS DEAD SON DURING A TELEVISED SEANCE

On September 3, 1967, Episcopal Bishop James A. Pike heard spirit messages, which he considered to be from his deceased son, through the mediumship of the Reverend Arthur Ford, an ordained minister of the Disciples of Christ Church. This particular seance, which took place in Toronto, Ontario, Canada, was unique in that it was not limited to a drape-darkened room, but was taped and broadcast on CTV, the private Canadian television network. Allen Spraggett, the man who had arranged the televised seance, was a former pastor of the United Church of Canada, and religion editor of the *Toronto Star*.

On September 17, the program was televised, and it precipitated the greatest furor that psychical research had experienced in many years. The controversial bishop, who was frequently spotlighted in the news for his dispute with the church over interpretation of certain traditional doctrines, stood his ground as firmly on the matter of communication with the dead as he had on other emotion-charged religious issues. He had, he told newsmen, spoken directly with his son, James A. Pike, Jr., through Arthur Ford, with the aid of the medium's customary spirit control, Fletcher.

In February, 1966, Bishop Pike's son had committed suicide at the age of twenty-two. The clergyman recalled that shortly after his son's death, he had, on several occasions, found pins paired together simulating clock hands indicating the time of James, Jr.'s suicide.

During the seance, Bishop Pike stated, his son's spirit had " . . . referred to events—a lot of difficulties—and seemed very aware of things."

Even before receiving the communication from his son during the seance, Bishop Pike had expressed belief in the possibility of contacting the dead. Before the televised seance, in answer to a direct question on the subject, he responded by saying that he firmly believed in life after death. He also held that " . . . on occasion there can be communication with those beyond the living."

It was "Fletcher," Arthur Ford's spirit control, who brought forth the bishop's son and other communicating personalities. Fletcher claims to have been a boyhood friend of Ford. For many years, the spirit control had brought forth third-person messages from the Next World through the entranced medium.

During the televised seance, Reverend Ford explained that he would go into a trance or a sleep. He placed a dark handkerchief over his eyes, commenting that it was easier to go to sleep if one did not have the light, and the bright lights of the television studio would make the acquisition of the trance state that much more difficult.

"So many people associate all this [spirit communication] with dark rooms," Reverend Ford said, "so I'll leave you in the light . . . anything that takes place in the dark can usually take place in the light."

Once Reverend Ford had attained the trance state, Fletcher soon made an appearance. Fletcher said that he had two people eager to speak with others who were waiting.

The first communicating entity was that of a young man who had been mentally disturbed and confused before he departed. The spirit being revealed itself as James A. Pike, Jr. He spoke of how happy he was to be able to talk to his father.

Next Fletcher introduced George Zobrisky, a lawyer who had taught history at Virginia Theological Seminary. Zobrisky said that he had "more or less shaped" Bishop Pike's thinking, a point which the clergyman readily conceded.

Louis Pitt then sent greetings to the clergyman. Bishop Pike recognized Pitt as having served as acting chaplain at Columbia University before Pike became chairman of the Department of Religion.

The fourth spirit entity to be brought into the seance was described by Fletcher as an "old gentleman who lectured." Fletcher added that the man had the same name as his father, a Scottish name. "The old man had two cats, which had formerly belonged to his son. And there was something about Corpus Christi."

Bishop Pike commented that there was a college at Cambridge by that name.

Spraggett, the host of the televised seance, asked Fletcher if he could provide a name.

The spirit control answered that the name sounded something like " . . . McKenny . . . McKennon . . . Donald McKennon."

Donald *McKinnon*, Bishop Pike confirmed, had been the principal influence on his thinking at Cambridge.

The last spirit to come forward during the seance told Fletcher that he had called himself an "ecclesiastical panhandler" in life.

Bishop Pike seemed to know at once what man had applied such an appellation to himself, but Spraggett once again asked the spirit control for a name.

"Oh," answered Fletcher, "something like Black. Carl. Carl Black . . . Block."

"Carl Block," Bishop Pike agreed, "the fourth bishop of California, my predecessor. I admired and respected you, and yet I hoped that you weren't feeling too badly about some changes."

Speaking through Fletcher, Bishop Block told

his successor that he had done " . . . a magnificent job, and you have magnificent work yet to do."

Bishop Pike later told the Associated Press that he did not see how any research done by Reverend Ford could have developed such intimate details about his life and such facts about the roles that certain individuals had played in shaping his thinking. The clergyman felt that the details had been " . . . quite cumulative. They are not just bits and pieces, an assortment of facts. They add together. They make a pattern."

In addition to the force of undying love that enabled his son to make contact with him, Bishop Pike noted that all of the other communicating entities had one thing in common: "They were in varying ways connected with the development of my thought. They knew me at particularly significant times in my life—turning points."

29

Mother Gave Them a Glowing Sign of Her Passing

Elaine Mitsuyoshi remembered so vividly the great pleasure that her mother-in-law Eva expressed when Tom, Elaine's husband, transformed an old rusted railroad lantern into a beautiful piece of art. Knowing that his mother had purchased the lantern at a yard sale several years before and had forgotten all about it, Tom had retrieved it from her basement and took it back to his own workshop.

"You have your father's talent for seeing the unusual and the lovely in the ordinary and the ugly," Eva Mitsuyoshi had said with pride. "Who would have thought that when you found this rusty old thing in the basement that you would make of it such a magnificent object of light."

Tom had spent several evenings working on the lantern. He had sanded off the rust, restored its bright red painted surface, then wired it and installed a bulb strategically behind the old wick. To top off his efforts, he had painted small scenes of railroad and frontier history on the base of the lamp.

"I know that I gave it to you," his mother teased. "But now that you have done such a good job on it, I think I want it back."

Tom laughed good-naturedly and gallantly offered to return it to his mother. Eva smiled and admitted that she was only being mischievous. "Besides," she added, "it is really too splendid to fit in with my glass turtles and ceramic animals. Let us say that it will be something to remember me by."

Tom immediately protested that he had far more wonderful things than an old lantern by which to remember his mother.

"I had a strange feeling when she made such a statement," Elaine said. "Although Mother Mitsuyoshi was in her early eighties, she was very healthy and spry. I couldn't remember her having a sick day. She still lived a very active life, and she gloried in her six children and all the activities of her twenty grandchildren. It seemed such a peculiar thing to say about the lantern."

In spite of Mrs. Mitsuyoshi's vigorous lifestyle, less than a month later she suffered a massive stroke.

"For nearly two weeks, her indomitable spirit struggled to continue life on the earth plane," Elaine stated. "Eva lay in a bed in the intensive care unit of the hospital, moving back and forth over a narrow line between life and death. Tom and her other children were fearful that the stroke might leave her paralyzed or otherwise physically impaired. While they wanted their mother with them forever, they were stricken with even greater grief when they considered a scenario that would see their once active mother spending her last days as a virtual vegetable on a life support system.

"On the fourteenth day after her stroke, the doctors told the family that Mother was doing so well that she could be transferred from the intensive care unit into a regular room and that she could begin to receive visits from her friends."

"Our prayers have been answered," Tom said on their drive home from the hospital. "We have our mother with us for a while longer, and she will soon be able to resume her normal pattern of activities."

Elaine and Tom had a quiet dinner with their two small sons, then decided to retire early for some much needed sleep.

"I was still operating on too much adrenalin to drop right off to sleep, so I decided I would read until I got drowsy enough to turn out the lights," Elaine recalled. "Because I enjoy reading in bed at night, Tom had placed the fancy refinished railroad lantern on my side of the bed. It was just the perfect height for me to read comfortably without disturbing his slumber."

Elaine had not read for more than fifteen or twenty minutes, when she heard the two boys begin to shout and the older of their sons cry out,

"Mommy, Daddy, what's that weird light doing out in the hallway?"

As she and Tom watched in astonishment a glowing ball of orange light, about the size of a baseball and moving in a zigzag pattern, floated into their bedroom. It hovered over the two of them for a second or two, then dove for the old railroad lantern and exploded with such force that the boys heard the sound in their bedroom and came running in fear to their parents.

On a soul-level of awareness, Tom knew that his mother had passed on. "Elaine," he said, his voice unsteady. "Oh, my God, I know that Mama has just been here to give us a sign that she has died."

Elaine put an arm around her husband's trembling shoulders to comfort him. She found herself speaking as if to convince herself as well as Tom. "Dear, you know that we left the hospital only a few hours ago. You know that Mother has made giant strides toward a recovery."

Tom shook his head in contradiction to her reassuring words. "Elaine, I know that Mama was just here to say good-bye. You know that the old lantern was the last thing she gave us. You remember the fuss that she made when I refinished it. Somehow, she was able to project her spiritual love so that it could connect with the last physical gift of her love."

Elaine stated that they learned later that Eva Mitsuyoshi had slipped into a coma just a few minutes before the manifestation of the glowing ball of light in their home. She died only two hours later.

"Tom will always feel, and I must agree, that his mother did in fact visit us to say a last farewell, and that that lantern over which he had so lovingly labored had somehow served as the catalyst to empower such a final thrust of physical energy from her dying brain," Elaine Mitsuyoshi said.

30

Her Sister's Spirit Freed Her From Suicidal Depression

When Claudia Epstein's twenty-four-year-old sister Nan and her husband, Daniel Moore, were killed in an airplane crash on September 12, 1988, she felt as if she no longer had any motivation to continue living.

"Our mother died when Nan and I were very young," Claudia said. "I was nine and Nan was only four. I guess that I became her surrogate mother, and our relationship had always been closer than most sisters that I knew. Dad didn't remarry until I was out of high school and in my second year of college, so I had a lot of years of looking out for Nan."

Claudia had been delighted when Nan and Dan had begun dating during their sophomore year in high school. "Dan was a hard-working, decent guy from a good family. I knew that this would be one of those high school romances that would last forever."

Sometimes, Claudia learned to her sorrow, "forever" on the earth plane may not last for a very long period of time.

"Nan and Dan were such a wonderful couple," she said. "They both got jobs right out of school and began to save for their marriage. Dan went to night school at a local junior college, and he was determined to better himself."

The always-practical young couple did not go on a honeymoon immediately after their wedding in May. They put it off until September so they would better be able to afford it.

"It was during takeoff of their honeymoon flight that the small commuter plane crashed," Claudia stated. "It was supposed to take them to a larger airport where they would take off for Tahiti. Instead, it rose just high enough to take them and seven other passengers to their deaths."

Claudia entered a period of deep depression after the fatal accident. "For a time, I sincerely felt that I could not go on living. My sister had become my world. My own plans for marriage had been dashed when my fiance was involved in a serious automobile accident and left mentally impaired. I had compensated for the loss of my future by lavishing even more emotional energy on Nan and Dan."

Although she had sought help from her rabbi, her parents, her doctor, and her friends, Claudia could find no respite from her sorrow. "I barely slept. Even my dreams were haunted with scenes of the crash and my deep sense of loss."

Claudia is now ashamed to admit that she had even considered suicide. "I felt that since they had been taken from me, I would join them on the other side. Thank God, I had confessed such a plan to my rabbi, and he convinced me that such a drastic deed would not produce the desired results."

Three months after the tragedy, shortly before the Hanukkah/Christmas season, Claudia left her home to seek rest and seclusion in a small ski resort in northern Colorado. "There was no way that I could deal with the holidays in the old familiar places where Nan and I had spent the previous two decades of wonderful holiday excitement, so I found this little out-of-the-way lodge where I could seek solace of spirit."

One night as she sat reading near the fireplace, Claudia unmistakably felt a physical presence behind her. "I turned to see Nan and Dan standing behind me in the center of the room. I saw them as solidly as I had ever seen them. They were smiling and holding hands. For the first time in months, I smiled also."

"Please do not continue to grieve so for us, dear one," Nan said in her familiar, soft, lilting voice. "Dan and I are now happier than ever. Our love is even stronger here than it was on earth."

"Why. . . . why did you have to leave me?" Claudia wanted to know. Fighting back the tears, she blurted out, "I can't go on without you."

"Of course you can, Big Sis," Nan admonished her. "You know, when you would leave me when I was just a little girl, I didn't think I could live without you. But you always came back home, and we were always together again. One day you will join us here, and the three of us will be together again. Until that day, dear, be happy and live a life of joy and fulfillment."

Before Claudia could speak again, Nan and Dan faded from sight—but the impact of Nan's words have never left.

"The proof of my sister's immortality freed me from my deep depression," Claudia said. "And the fact that she appeared to be happy permitted me to be positive about life once again. All of my family members and friends were pleased to notice my new attitude when I came home after the holidays. To all who would listen, I told the story of a sister's love that was able to push aside the dark curtain of physical death long enough to restore the faith of one who had felt left behind to survive only in gloom and despair. To all who would listen, I declared that love is the greatest power in the universe."

31

Consolation and Popcorn
From the Other Side

When Ravelle Lynch's husband, Alan, died of cancer in April of 1990, she knew that he would contact her from beyond the grave.

"Of course I felt deep grief for my loss," she said, "but I also was sustained by a profound 'knowing' that Alan would communicate with me."

When Alan's doctor first discovered what appeared to be early signs of cancer, he ordered an extensive battery of laboratory tests. Everyone breathed a sigh of relief and offered prayers of thanks when the tests came back negative. Then, four months later, Alan was diagnosed in the advanced stages of lymphatic cancer and given only weeks to live. The test results had somehow been confused with another's. The laboratory technicians said that they were sorry.

Alan and Ravelle spent as much of their remaining hours together as possible, and they spoke much of spiritual matters and the afterlife. Masking his pain with a broad grin, Alan helped make his coming transition less traumatic for their children, twelve-year-old Laura and ten-year-old Louis.

"Alan had always been a deeply religious man," Ravelle said, "although in later years we had not been as active in formal, organized religion. Alan, especially, had found increasing peace in reading the works of certain of the early New England transcendentalists, such as Emerson and Thoreau."

Ravelle also noted that Alan had been a regular reader of the Bible since his adolescence. "We often had evening Bible study with the entire family, and Alan always read several passages from the New Testament before going to sleep at night."

Alan met death fearlessly. "He had been reading the Bible aloud until his poor voice had become no more than a rasping whisper. Then he set the good book aside and asked me to sit nearer the bed. 'I will always be with you, darling,' he said. 'I will always love you.' He gave me one last smile, then closed his eyes in the perfect peace that passes all understanding."

Shortly after his passing, Ravelle was aware of an occasional light tap on her shoulder or on her back. "These loving touches would come at times when I felt especially lonely and sad. I understand that the skeptic might remain unconvinced, but

I knew that those soft, affectionate pats on the back were Alan's unique and special way of giving me encouragement to continue the struggle of life and to provide me with proof that he was still at my side."

Although Ravelle received sign after sign that Alan was contented in his new dimension and still in contact with the earth plane, she grew increasingly concerned about Laura.

"Laura had been very close to her father," Ravelle said. "She was truly a daddy's girl. She had always been an exceptionally healthy and robust girl, very athletic and sports-minded; but now, after Alan's death, she barely nibbled at her food. She seemed to lose interest in her school work, and she seldom bothered to return the telephone calls of her friends. She would sit for hours in front of the television set, but it was obvious that she wasn't really watching it."

After nearly four months of such behavior, Laura had become a pale shadow of her former self. Although she had scarcely wept or shown any outward sign of grief, it was apparent that she had been devastated by her father's death.

"One night, after my evening prayers, I looked at Alan's picture beside the bed and asked aloud that he help our daughter to accept his passing," Ravelle admitted. "I told Alan that it had to be up to him to console her, to make her understand that he was still with us in spirit."

Four days later, the morning after her thirteenth birthday, Laura came to the breakfast table and asked for a bowl of oatmeal and some toast with peanut butter. She had a second bowl of cereal before she left for school.

"I gave thanks to God and a special wink to Alan," Ravelle said. "I was curious as to what had occurred, but I kept quiet for several days, just rejoicing in the fact that Laura's appetite and good spirits had returned."

About a week later, as Ravelle sat mending some of the children's clothing, Laura came to her and somewhat hesitantly asked if she could tell her something very important. "Daddy came to see me the night of my birthday," she said, speaking each word very softly and distinctly.

Laura studied her mother's face, not certain if she would find acceptance or rejection of the reality of the visitation. When Ravelle neither laughed nor scolded her, but indicated that she should continue, Laura became quite enthusiastic.

"Oh, Mommy," she said, "it was Daddy, I know it was. He came in through the door just after I went to bed, and he pulled the covers up under my chin, just the way he used to. And he bent down and kissed me and called me 'Kitten' and wished me a happy birthday."

Ravelle felt tears stinging her eyes. "Did your daddy say anything else, honey?"

Laura nodded her head vigorously. "He told me that he was doing just fine where he was, but he said that he was so sad that I was feeling so miserable about his dying and all. He told me that I should read the Bible more and to ask you to tell me the names of some of the books that you used to read together. Daddy said that I could understand them now . . . and that if I didn't, he would help me."

Ravelle understood at once the books of devotion to which Alan must have referred. She would also begin to read certain inspirational works aloud to the children, and they would plan a nightly Bible reading.

"Daddy told me that even though we live in two separate worlds now, he is still close to me and to Louis and to you," Laura continued. "He said that even though it might be hard for me to understand, it only *seemed* as though he was far, far away. He was really always right beside me in another kind of dimension. And he said that even though I might not always be able to see him, he would help me throughout life. And, best of all, he said that he loved me . . . all of us . . . just as much as before."

Laura put her arms around her mother's shoulders and began to weep openly and without restraint. It was truly the first time that she had released the terrible grief which she had kept bottled so tightly within her young body.

Ravelle was cradling her daughter in her arms, saying a silent blessing to Alan's memory when Louis suddenly burst into the room.

"It's daddy's popcorn! Smell it? It's daddy's popcorn!" he shouted over and over.

It took Ravelle a few moments to make any kind of sense of Louis' bizarre chanting. And then she, too, detected the fragrant and homey aroma of freshly popped, buttered popcorn.

"It is," Laura was smiling, wiping away tears with the back of a hand. "Smell it, Mommy. That's Daddy's famous popcorn."

Although Alan had absolutely no culinary talents and freely admitted to his adult friends that he could barely boil water without burning it, he loved to make popcorn for the kids on nights when they could stay up a bit later and watch a movie or a television special together. He would make up elaborate stories of secret old Lynch family recipes for the ultimate popcorn, and he had even fabricated an account of receiving an Olympic medal for his popcorn prowess.

"We all smelled it," Ravelle said. "The aroma of freshly buttered popcorn was coming from the kitchen and permeating the entire house. It was the scent of Alan's 'world famous popcorn,' and we all breathed its glorious smell as deeply as we could.

"The aroma of popcorn lasted for about three or four minutes, then it was gone as quickly as it had come. But the memory of that wonderful moment of contact from beyond the grave will stay with my children and me until the day that we each of us, in our own time, rejoin our loving husband and father. In his own special way, Alan had given us a communication that we could all share and understand."

32

A Kiss of Forgiveness

When Walter Becker passed away on January 12, 1987, his wife, Janete, was left with feelings of numbing grief coupled with unresolved guilt.

"We had been married for over twenty years," she said, "but during the last four years of his life, Walter had been very ill. The pleasant man that I had married had long ago been absorbed into a man of pain and discontent. His once even disposition had been replaced by a temperament that was easily irritated and could blaze forth on a moment's notice into awful temper tantrums over the most minute of circumstances."

Janete had been patient and long-suffering for quite some time, but she did not hold herself blameless. "There were occasions when I felt so annoyed with his foul moods and so ill-treated by his nasty words and insults, that I struck back with nasty words and cruel barbs of my own."

On the night following Walter's death, Janete lay in an awful sleeplessness, tortured with thoughts of their life together. There had been so many good times in the beginning of their marriage. Why couldn't the memories of those happy days have somehow sustained her during the trying days of Walter's painfully debilitating illness?

"Death can be a stern teacher," Janete said. "Death presents too many lessons that are too late to correct. I saw so clearly how faulty human judgments can be. I perceived with great sorrow how a quickly and harshly uttered word can leave an indelible impression in the psyche. Most of all I realized how Walter's irascibility was a result of his lingering illness, and I felt a terrible guilt for not having the strength of soul to remain more patient."

Janete had begun to sob aloud in her despair when she distinctly felt a kiss on her left cheek. "I sat up quickly in bed and saw the faint form of Walter standing beside me. He was smiling, and looked much as he had shortly after we were first married. As I sat bolt upright in astonishment, he leaned forward and kissed me once again on the left cheek. I felt that kiss, calm and cool, as vividly as I had ever felt it in his living form. And then Walter's image vanished.

"But his smile and his kisses had told me that he, too, understood the reasons for our strained relationship during his final days. He had forgiven me, and now I must forgive him—and myself."

Janete said that once more the following day when a guilt pang had crept up on her, she sensed again a loving, forgiving kiss on her cheek.

"I am well aware that so many in our present materialistic and skeptical world will have a dozen theories that would seek to explain away my kiss of forgiveness from Walter," she remarked. "But as for me, the sensation was too real, too genuine, too filled with pure love for me to doubt."

33

"Everything Is All Right Now!"

When Diana Korey awakened on that chilly November morning of 1983, she arose with an acute sensation that something was very wrong. As she prepared breakfast, she carefully examined her fourteen-year-old son Kevin and her nine-year-old daughter Patty.

"Since they seemed well and happy, I knew then that it had to be my husband, Marc, who was institutionalized in the big veterans' hospital nearly 200 miles away."

Marc, a Vietnam veteran, suffered from a progressive disease that he had contracted while in the service. He had dealt courageously with his illness, but in the spring of 1981, the stresses of rearing a family, adjusting to society, and combatting a steadily debilitating disease had combined to bring about a nervous breakdown. Tragically, Marc had succumbed to a more complex mental illness after he had nearly recovered from the shattering of his nerves.

Diana went to work that November morning feeling extremely distracted and ill-at-ease. "I was lucky my boss didn't fire me. I was continually drifting off into thoughts of great concern for Marc."

That evening when she returned home, she was no longer able to contain herself. She knew that it was always difficult to get through to someone of authority in the veterans' hospital, but she also knew that she must try to do so in order to set her mind at ease.

At last she managed to be put through to the extension of an exceedingly ill-mannered doctor who informed her that her husband's condition remained unchanged. "Furthermore," the doctor grumbled, "Mr. Korey's condition is not likely to change for several months, perhaps years. You will just have to content yourself with the knowledge that he is well cared for and that we are doing the best we can . . . under the circumstances."

The doctor's brusque asssurances of Marc's condition being the best that it could be "under the circumstances" did nothing to calm Diana's concern. In fact, the words so professionally designed to pacify her had achieved the opposite effect. She felt all the more convinced that something was wrong with Marc.

"After the kids were in bed, I retreated to my own private altar that I had constructed in a corner of my bedroom," she said. "I read from the Psalms, the New Testament, then lighted some candles and incense and began to pray. After a period of intense meditation, I soaked in a warm tub and went to bed."

Diana was awakened from a sound sleep by the voice of her husband calling her by his pet nickname for her: "Hey, Tiger Lily, wake up!"

"Marc's voice brought me awake with a choked cry of joy.

"Perhaps I was in that in-between space between wakefulness and sleep, for I felt there was nothing strange about his standing firm and solid at my bedside. As I reached out to touch him, I asked with an inner knowing, 'You're all right now, aren't you, Marc?' "

Diana's fingertips touched the firm flesh of Marc's hand, and he closed his own fingers tightly around them. "Yes, honey," he replied. "Everything is all right now. Always remember that I loved you so very much. Kiss the kids good-bye."

And then he disappeared. Diana's hand now clutched only a memory.

She turned on the light and took careful note of the time on her clock radio. It was 2:08 A.M.

"I had no doubt that the visitation that I had just experienced was the result of my husband's death," she said. "I knew that Marc had come to say good-bye."

She was so certain that she had correctly interpreted Marc's spectral visit that she began to plan to leave for the hospital. She would get her mother to watch the kids. She would call her boss's answering machine at dawn to inform him that she would not be at work for a few days.

She had already fixed the children's breakfast when the official call came from the veterans' hospital at 7:30 A.M. A more sympathetic sounding doctor expressed his condolences, then informed her that Marc had died at about two o'clock that morning. Melanoma metastic to the brain had snuffed out his life.

"He died at 2:08, to be precise," Diana said aloud, not really knowing why it felt so important to correct the doctor.

There was a moment of awkward silence, then the doctor wanted to know if someone—an *authorized* someone—had called her earlier.

"None of your staff disobeyed your orders not to call me until 7:30," Diana said. "I'm nearly ready to leave for the drive for the hospital. I'll explain it to you when I see you."

It was on that long journey to the veterans' hospital that Diana once again heard Marc's voice.

"He told me that he was now free, free of pain, free of confusion. And he told me that we would always be together on some level of a greater reality. I know that he has always looked after our children's welfare from his dimension of being, and I have felt his loving presence in my own life on many occasions."

34

Rick Came Home for Christmas

The Horton family buried Rick, their son, husband, and father on December 4, 1977. A sudden heart attack had taken him from his wife Melba, his three young children, and his loving parents, Louise and Charles.

"Rick would have been 38 years old the day before Christmas," Louise said, "and in spite of the heavy cloud of grief that hung over us, Charlie and I decided that we would do everything that we could to make the remainder of the Christmas Holiday just as happy as possible. We knew that Rick would have wanted it that way."

Louise and Charles set about decorating the house, inside and out, just as they had since Rick was a small boy. They made certain that Melba and the kids knew that they were to come for a big turkey dinner on Christmas Eve and that they would go to church as a family on Christmas Day. Everything would be just as it would have been if Rick had not died.

As Louise and Charles were assembling the miniature manager scene that they had placed on the fireplace mantle ever since Rick was seven years old, it came to them to fashion a small home altar to commemorate their son.

"We bought a terrarium to honor Rick's love of plants and nature," Louise stated. "Charles filled a tall, purple-tinted urn with scented water. Around Rick's picture, we placed a tall red candle in a bright green holder and a number of Christmas tree ornaments to add the touch of holiday color that he had always loved so very much. Just off to the left side, we placed a small incense burner in which we burned cones of sandalwood three or four times a day."

Solemnly, just a few days before Christmas, Charles lighted the tall red candle, and Louise lay an open Bible on the altar. Both of them gave silent prayers toward the same unspoken request: That they be given a sign that Rick's spirit was a happy one.

Louise began to cry softly, then lowered her head against Charles' shoulder.

"Don't cry, Mom," he comforted her, taking one of her hands in his own. "If there is any way between heaven and earth for Rick to make contact with us, you know that he will find it."

Louise smiled. Charlie had tried to tame their son's assertive personality when he was a boy, but he had come to admire Rick's aggressiveness. Rick had the knack of knowing when to turn on the charm and when to push for what he wanted. He had used this balance of talents successfully through high school, college, and the business world. If only he hadn't been taken from his family when he was so young. . . .

"You know, Mom," Charlie was chuckling, "there wasn't anything on this whole planet that that boy couldn't figure out. If there is a way to bring us a message, you know he will. I'll bet at this very minute he's lecturing the angels on how to do their jobs more efficiently."

On Christmas Eve day, Louise was up early to begin to prepare a hearty meal for the family. Melba and the children would arrive around five o'clock for an early dinner. Everyone would have to help clean up the kitchen, then it would be the kids' time to open the presents under the tree. Then, as they had planned it, Melba and the grandkids would stay over night so that they could all attend early church services the next morning.

Melba and the children arrived a bit early, just a little after four.

"I sometimes get a bit nervous and jumpy when I feel that I am pressured," Louise admitted. "I knew the kids would start snooping around the presents and be getting into things they shouldn't. Charlie was still reading the evening paper, so I knew that he wouldn't be doing much policing of his grandkids. Melba asked if she could help fill the relish trays and so forth, but I'm fussy about finishing things that I start.

"So what I am saying," Louise said emphatically, "is that *normally* the music coming from the radio wouldn't have bothered me, but right then, it was getting on my nerves."

Louise waited to speak until she knew that she was calm enough not to shout. "Charlie, I love Christmas carols as much as the next person, but could we do without them for a little while?"

Her husband gave her one of his famous blank looks. "What do you mean, Mom?"

Louise took his question to signal resistance to her subtle request to shut off the radio. Her voice was just a bit louder, not really sharp—she hoped: "At least until I finish preparing dinner, *please* shut off the radio."

"Mom," her husband said quietly, "there is no radio or television set on in this house at this moment."

And then they all began to pay attention to the music that was filtering through the house. It was a lovely haunting melody, strangely familiar, yet none of them could identify it.

"It sounds kind of Christmas-like," Melba offered her opinion, "but it is no hymn or holiday song that I know."

Louise remembered that they looked everywhere for the source of the beautiful melody. "There's sometimes a chorus of voices with it . . . like angels," she said to the others.

Charles had even gone outside to see if a car had parked nearby with its radio left playing. The music was not issuing from any source that they could locate.

"And then, I suppose, we began to move to the one place that we had all, on one level of awareness, been avoiding," Louise stated. "We began to move toward the altar that we had prepared to commemorate Rick's passing."

Melba began to weep as the entire family, including the children, heard the ethereal music coming from the ornaments around Rick's photograph. "He always loved music," she said softly.

"Always did," Charles agreed, his eyes misting with tears. "Seldom went without music wherever he was."

And then, just as suddenly as it had begun, the music stopped.

"The radio!" Louise suddenly had a clearer picture of what was occurring on that remarkable Christmas Eve, the birthday of their son. "I wanted the radio off. *Rick wants the radio on!*"

Charles clicked on the old console model they still kept in the living room. The very first sounds that flowed from the radio were the words from the poignant holiday song that promises, "I'll be home for Christmas."

"We all stood there, tears flowing freely, unchecked," Louise said. "We all hugged each other and those of us who knew the words sang along with the radio."

"I told you Rick would find a way," Charles said, laughing and crying at the same time. "He did it. Rick came home for Christmas"

And, Louise concluded, her son had brought his family the greatest Christmas gift possible. "He demonstrated the truth of the Christmas promise for all of his family. He gave his children a proof of life eternal that will strengthen them all the days of their lives."

35

Can Mediums Contact Our Loved Ones in the Spirit World?

The multi-talented Whoopi Goldberg won an academy award for best supporting actress for her role as the Spiritualist medium who becomes the reluctant channel for Patrick Swayze's anxious spirit in the popular 1990 motion picture *Ghost*. The position of the spirit medium in our culture has varied from the much-acclaimed to the much-maligned.

Certain readers will immediately question whether or not any living person can claim regular contact with those on the Other Side. To most of those reared in religious or scientific orthodoxy, the very idea that one claims to be able to contact the deceased is equivalent to saying that one is a fraud and a charlatan. It is one thing to hear of someone's personal account of having received some kind of communication from the dearly departed that has occurred naturally, unprovoked, unsought; but it is quite another to hear of someone who can deliberately communicate with those in the spirit world.

And yet in many cases, the results seem to be the same: The precious proof of the undying love of their spouse, sweetheart, parent, or child. And although the term "spirit medium" is a scarey term for some people, it is really quite descriptive. After all, scientists now tell us that with our five senses we are able to apprehend less than one percent of all the various energies that surround us. Perhaps somewhere in that other 99% of swirling frequencies, messages are being sent all around us on a regular basis, but we are unable to receive them. It might just be that some people have the ability to become attuned to certain frequencies that others of us do not perceive.

"There was no possibility of my simply being gullible," Sam Crawford told us after a visit to a professional medium. "The medium told me things about Lily that only I would know. If I had not been crying so with tears of joy, I might have been embarrassed in front of the other sitters at the seance. I mean, the medium, the channeler, revealed some extremely intimate details of our love life that were completely accurate."

WHO BECOMES A SPIRIT MEDIUM?

What kind of person becomes a medium? The skeptics immediately nominate the "odd" or poorly adjusted members of society as their candidates for the role of psychic sensitive or medium. The cynics add that the general level of intelligence among mediums must be very low.

The first thing one learns when one begins an investigation of mediumship is that mediums are people. They are nurses, accountants, ministers, journalists, real estate agents, advertising executives, schoolteachers, housewives, farmers—in short, one finds as wide a range of occupations among mediums as he would find among lefthanded people or folks with red hair. Few mediums are full-time professionals.

As far as social adjustment is concerned, psychical researchers have found that those individuals who are well-adjusted socially and who are possessed of an extroverted rather than an introverted personality are the ones who score higher in ESP tests. The same may be said of mediums. One consistently encounters the enthusiastic extrovert rather than the moody or misanthropic introvert.

There is no conclusive evidence to indicate that high or low intelligence contributes to either ESP abilities or mediumistic sensitivity. Again, one seems to find generally average to high-average intelligence among mediums. Certainly not the low IQ dullards that some people like to consider as being representative of someone who likes to talk to spirits.

WHAT IS THE SOURCE OF MEDIUMISTIC KNOWLEDGE?

Certain researchers have come to concede a high degree of accuracy to the better of the professional mediums, but they tend to attribute the source of such information to little known powers of mind, rather than to surviving spirit communicators. These investigators would say that the only difference between a psychic "sensitive" and a spiritistic medium is that the psychic attributes his unusual talents to some manifestation of ESP ability, *i.e.* clairvoyance, precognition, telepathy; whereas the medium claims his revelations are a result of the interaction of spirit entities.

Those of us who have witnessed, under test conditions, any of the physical phenomena of the seance room must acknowledge the functioning of a dynamic force capable of moving heavy objects without physical contact, materializing ectoplasmic forms and phantoms, and providing information which could not have been learned by the medium through the normal channels of sensory impressions.

Those of us who have observed such phenomena must also affirm that this force, whatever it may be and from whatever source it may emanate, possesses an intelligence. The spiritistic hypothesis holds that this intelligence originates from spirits of the dead.

Perhaps a majority of psychical researchers accept the phenomena but deny the alleged source. These same investigators maintain that this as yet undefinable force emanates from the living, that is, from the medium and, perhaps, from the combined psyches of the medium and the sitters.

Certain serious researchers have expressed their opinion that the intelligence exhibited by the "spirits" is most often on a level with that of the medium through which they manifest themselves. These same investigators admit that the information relayed often rises far above the medium's known objective intelligence, but they are quick to point out that the limits of the subjective mind are not yet known.

THE RULES OF SPIRITUAL ETIQUETTE WHEN VISITING A MEDIUM

If you, the reader, have not been given messages from your departed loved ones and you sincerely desire contact, we suggest first that you give the matter some very serious prayer and ask God to help you to listen and to tune in to higher levels of awareness.

If you find that your religious orthodoxy gets in the way, it might help you as it did us to consider that God can work through a spirit medium if it is for your good and your gaining that you receive a message from the next world. Indeed, the spirits who present the mediums their messages may be angels whose function is exactly that of messengers. Hebrews 1:14 says, "Are they not all ministering spirits sent forth to minister for them who shall be heirs of salvation?"

We feel that you, the seeker of spirit contact, should first exhaust every natural means of establishing communication through prayers and quiet time in the silence of your inner self. We also recognize that, occasionally, one might find that there are too many emotional stumbling blocks, and some assistance may be required.

Should you decide to attend a session with a professional medium to judge such spiritistic claims for yourself, you should be certain to give the medium to understand that you, as a sitter, are assured of the medium's honesty and his or her ability to produce genuine information. You should not hurry the medium, but allow the channel to take all the time that he or she wishes. You, as a neophyte sitter, should remember that the greatest guarantee of a successful session is the medium's serene state of mind.

As a psychical researcher, one soon learns that the best manner in which to obtain a demonstration of genuine spiritistic phenomena is to assure the medium of one's good will. When one has the confidence of the medium, one has accomplished an indispensable prerequisite to the production of genuine phenomena.

If you should attend a seance in which no phenomena is produced, you should not conclude that the medium is therefore dishonest. Neither psychicism nor true spirit contact is easily turned on or off like a television set or a radio.

Until the mental and spiritual laws governing this kind of phenomena are better understood, it would seem not only charitable but just to reserve the charges of trickery and chickanery for those instances in which gimmicked paraphernalia have been found to have been prepared by the medium in advance of the seance with the deliberate intention to defraud.

It must be pointed out that the vast majority of spirit mediums consider their ability to communicate with the deceased as an expression of their religious belief system. The sincere medium is no more a fraud than the sincere pastor, priest, or rabbi. The serious medium sees himself or herself has one who has broken free of the mechanistic psychology of a materialistic society to exercise a God-given ability to establish contact with the dead.

Many psychical researchers will speak to that assertion by suggesting that the subjective mind of the medium operates under the suggestion that it is being controlled by the spirit of a deceased person. In other words, the medium has conditioned his or her subjective mind to the pervading premise by his education, environment, and religious beliefs.

THE TRANCE STATE

When a medium enters the trance state, he or she enters into a subjective condition that leaves him as open and as amenable to the law of suggestion as is the subject of hypnosis. The potent suggestion that a spirit of the dead is about to enter his body and control him is ever present to the subjective mind of the medium. Such a suggestion has been a part of his or her educational development. His or her religious beliefs are based on the *fact* of spirit survival and communication. All phenomena are considered by the medium to be a direct interaction of the spirit world with the physical world. The trance state allows the medium to cooperate with extraneous personalities and become a vital link in the relaying of communication between the two worlds. The medium believes in survival and longs to establish contact with the loved ones of his or her own experience and to aid others in contacting their beloved. With such a powerful auto-suggestion constantly being directed to the transcendent level of his or her mind, all subjective knowledge gained by establishing *rapport* with the subconscious levels of other minds will be immediately interpreted as information gained by the intercession of spirits.

THE SPIRIT GUIDE

If you should decide to visit a spirit medium in an attempt to establish contact with a deceased loved one, you must also be aware of the medium's spirit guide. It is this alleged entity who will speak through the medium while he or she is in a trance state and will work all manner of mysterious phenomena on his or her behalf. Whether one accepts the entity as a true spirit or as the voice of the medium's subconscious, seance room etiquette requires one to address the guide courteously and in a manner which distinguishes the entity from the medium.

The great majority of mediums credit God and a spirit control as a dual source of their abilities.

Dr. William Thompson is the spirit guide of Mary E. Wing, a retired Spiritualist minister from Sacramento, California. "He was an Englishman, and he has been dead for over 400 years now. All those who have heard Dr. Thompson know that he is one of God's workers. He always gives beautiful and good advice."

Rev. Ralph McCallister of the Universal Temple of Truth Foundation in Huntington, West Virginia, says that he receives his blessings from five spirit guides—Adelia, Cleke, Pine Burr, Dr. Barnett, and his deceased son, Bill.

Marie Selleck of East Palo Alto, California, is another medium who looks to many guides for her inspiration. She names Dr. Reynolds, White Star, Big Drum, Dr. Rhodes, Quong Lee, a number of spirit children, and a nurse, Sister Mary.

Deon Frey, formerly of Chicago, one of the most powerful physical mediums in the United States, has worked in spirit with Dr. Richard Spiedel as a control for many years now.

The concept of a spirit guide dates back to antiquity and is known to all cultures. In our own Western historical context, the great philosopher

Socrates furnishes us with the most notable example in ancient times of a man whose subjective mind was able to communicate directly with his objective mind. Socrates referred to this inner voice as his guardian spirit, and he believed that it kept vigil over his activities and warned him of approaching danger.

Numerous psychical researchers have suggested that the spirit guide may be another as yet little known power of the mind, which enables the medium's subjective level of consciousness to dramatize another personality, complete with a full range of personal characteristics and its very own "voice."

The spiritistic medium looks at the spirit control in a very different manner. While a medium may concede that the action of the subjective mind is not entirely eliminated during the trance state and the arrival of the guide, he will assert that his subconscious is taken over by a discarnate entity.

Our research has informed us that the great majority of mediums have been spiritually "gifted" since childhood and most began an interaction with their spirit guides at a very early age.

"When I was around eleven or twelve, two guides would come to me nearly every night and lift me from my physical body," one medium told us. "As soon as I was out of the body, I would receive instruction from spirit teachers. I suppose you could say it was like going to night school, but I always used to awaken in the morning feeling completely refreshed."

EXAMINING THE LIFE OF
A GIFTED MEDIUM

The late Eileen Garrett was a gifted and wise medium who, until the time of her death, continued to study the phenomena of her mediumship in a manner that was incredibly detached and objective. Eileen Garrett had what we have come to recognize as a typical medium's childhood. She was ill a great deal and began to experience visions and to see "people" who were not there at a very early age.

She did not learn that she was a trance medium until she accidentally fell asleep at a public meeting, and the voices of the deceased relatives of those people sitting near her began to speak through her mouth. One man present explained to her what had happened and told her that he had been addressed by an entity claiming to be an Oriental spirit named Uvani, who would thereafter be her guide. According to her informant, the entity had said that he and Eileen Garrett would work together to prove the validity of the theory of the survival of the alleged dead.

Eileen was horrified at the prospect of sharing her body, her subconscious, and her life with an Oriental spirit. For weeks she slept with a night light burning in her room for fear that Uvani might put in a materialized appearance.

Later, a man at a London spiritualist society explained away her misgivings by assuring her that her spirit guide would not be at all interested in her daily life or her private experiences. Uvani's whole purpose was based on a sincere wish to be of service to humanity.

During the years in which she perfected her communication with her spirit guide, Eileen Garrett often expressed doubts about Uvani's spiritual independence and voiced a suspicion that he might only be a segment of her own subconscious mind. Such alternate theories were the dismay of the Spiritualists who were tutoring her with the utmost seriousness of purpose.

The brilliant psychical researcher Hereward Carrington devoted an entire book (*The Case for Psychic Survival*) to his examination of Eileen Garrett. He administered an extensive battery of personality tests to both Uvani and to Eileen so that researchers might compare the results of the two sets of responses. The spirit guide and the medium sat through sessions of the Bernreuter Personality Inventory, the Thurstone Attitude Scale, the Woodworth Neurotic Inventory, and Rorschach Test, and a seemingly endless number of word association tests.

Carrington concluded that even though there existed only slight scientific evidence for the genuinely spiritistic character of spirit guides such "entities" did succeed in bringing through vast amounts of "supernormal" information which "could not be obtained in their absence." The researcher declared that spirit guides appeared to act as some sort of "psychic catalizers."

Carrington goes on to theorize that the function of a medium's regular spirit guide seems to be that of an intermediary; and whether the entity is truly a spirit or a personification of the medium's subconscious, it is only through the cooperation of the guide that truthful and accurate messages can be obtained.

Making a sharp distinction between the secondary personalities sometimes observed in pathological cases, the researcher noted that in mediumistic cases, we have to deal with a personality which is somehow in touch or contact, in some mysterious way, with another world or dimension from which it derives information and genuine messages from the deceased.

A CONVERSATION WITH A SPIRIT GUIDE

In an interesting appendix to Carrington's book, he records a conversation with Uvani in which he questions the spirit guide concerning the mechanics involved in the controlling of Eileen Garrett's "underconscious" (the spirit guide's term for the subconscious).

Uvani emphasizes the fact that although he controls the medium's underconsciousness, he has absolutely no control over her conscious mind, nor would he consider such control to be right.

To the investigator's question of whether or not he has any knowledge of Eileen's mind, Uvani answers that he has no interest in her thoughts or in the activity of her conscious mind.

The trance state, to Uvani, is that time when he can make the medium's subconscious become a channel not only for his ideas but for many other entities. The underconsciousness, Uvani explained, is the vehicle on which his energy worked like notes upon a piano.

Carrington wondered how a spirit, such as Uvani, could perceive when a medium, such as Eileen, was ready to serve as a channel for communication.

Uvani answered that he received a "telegraphed impression" that the mediumistic "instrument" is ready: "The moment that the conscious mind becomes very low, then the soul-body becomes more vibrant. . . . But remember, it is prepared before I take command . . ."

The researcher was also curious to find out how an alleged Oriental spirit could speak such excellent English.

Uvani's immediate response was that he could not speak a word of English. "It is my instrument [Eileen Garrett] who speaks," the spirit guide explained. "I impress my thought upon her . . . but no word of mine actually comes to you. The instrument is impressed by my personal contact." Thoughts, Uvani goes on to elaborate, are impressed and expressed automatically through an entirely spiritual mechanism.

ARTHUR FORD AND "FLETCHER"

In his autobiography, written in collaboration with Marguerite Harmon Bro, the famous medium Arthur Ford clarified the working relationship which he enjoyed with his guide, Fletcher.

When he wished to go into trance, he said, he would lie down on a couch or lean back in a comfortable chair and breathe slowly and rhythmically until he felt an in-drawing of energy at his solar plexus. "Then I focus my attention on Fletcher's face as I have come to know it," Ford continued, "until gradually I feel as if his face presses into my own at which instant there is a sense of shock somewhat as if I were passing out." At that point, Ford said, he would lose consciousness. When he awakened at the end of a seance, it was as if he had had a "good nap."

THE POPULARITY OF INDIAN SPIRIT GUIDES

We have often asked mediums why so many spirit guides are American Indians or members of some other more primitive, less technological, culture. No one could help noticing that among professional mediums there seems to be a great preponderance of "Red Clouds," "Many Feathers," "Redwings," and other such Amerindian names.

The answers to this query vary little. The Indians, we have been told, maintained an essential relationship with natural forces and an undogmatic approach to the Spirit of Creation. This vital element, so common among Indians and other less technological peoples, seems to be woefully lacking in most of the spirit entities who arrive from a more civilized and materialistic era and locale.

AIDING TWO ACCIDENT VICTIMS TO FIND THE LIGHT

A psychic sensitive on the West Coast, whom we'll call Vanessa, told us of a time when she had to aid the recent dead in making the adjustment that must occur before the soul can accept its etheric condition.

"Two young men had been killed in a terrible automobile accident near our home." Vanessa said. "Not long after, I could sense their presence around me. I permitted myself go enter a light trance, and I could see them clearly.

"They were moving about wildly, in a state of panic. They had been so full of the world, so full of the desires of the flesh, so fired by their hopes for the future that they were totally confused by their present state of nonmateriality. It was apparent that while in the body they had neither one of them given much thought to spiritual matters, so now they were completely unprepared for what had happened to them."

Vanessa knew that since she was in the proximity of the accident, the two spirits had been drawn to her sensitivity just as iron filings to a magnet. "I felt that the angel guides of the two young men had directed them to me, because the guides, in their wisdom, had known that the recently deceased would not yet accept guidance from ethereal beings."

Vanessa tried to calm the two young men and to explain what had occurred to them. She told them that they must accept their entrance into the Greater Reality.

"For the longest time, they simply would not listen to me. Their thoughts were so filled with earthly desires and frustrations. They did not want to leave the earth plane. Their girlfriends were waiting for them. They had plans for their lives on earth, and they felt cheated to have their lives cut short. One of them was only twenty-two, the other, barely out of his teens.

"They were truly what is referred to as 'earth-bound spirits,'" Vanessa said. "They did not feel any of the peace that comes to most souls when they leave the earth plane."

At last she managed to calm the distressed and confused spirits enough so that their own guides could approach and remove them to another plane. "Suddenly the two men began to be pulled straight up. Such action on the part of the guides startled them, and they let out terrible screams of fear. There would still be much work for the angelic guides to accomplish, but at least I had aided the two men in their transference into the Light."

When Vanessa returned to full consciousness, she became aware that her tiny front room was filled with neighbors. "I lay on my couch, and one of my closest friends was bending over me and rubbing my wrists. They had all heard the terrible screams of the young men and had come to see if anything was wrong. I was amazed that they had been able to hear the screams that had come from the spirits, but I told them that I had just dozed off. I tried to blame the screams on the television set, which had been left on in my study. I don't know how many of my neighbors accepted this explanation, but they could certainly see that I was all alone in my little house."

THE REMARKABLE IRENE HUGHES

One of the most well-known and highly respected of today's mediums is Irene Hughes of Chicago. Intelligent, articulate, and perceptive as an individual and highly accurate as a channel and psychic sensitive, Irene has forthright answers for any sincere seeker of a doorway to another dimension.

It was on June 13, 1961, that Irene's spirit teacher first appeared to her. She was recovering from surgery when an Oriental gentleman materialized in her room. At first, she did not know if she were suffering from hallucinations or if she had died in surgery and not realized it.

The entity allowed Irene to test it, and promised to make three desires come to pass. When the spirit, who called himself "Kaygee" had seen to the fulfillment of these wishes, he led Irene back through a dramatic recall of a life spent in Egypt and predicted in what manner she would soon meet the other principals who had been with her in that prior life experience.

*   *   *

"I am your control, your teacher, and your friend," Kaygee told her. "You will learn many things unknown to others. You now have the key to all of life. Use it well, and it will grow. I will always be there to help you."

On one occasion, Kaygee held out a hand of friendship, and when Irene accepted it, she was startled to find it solid, warm, filled with life—although the air about the spirit entity was chilled.

Kaygee told her that he would teach her that love is truly the whole law of life, that " . . . love is the mightiest power in the universe, and you will learn this and teach this and lecture to people on this eternal truth. You will be given the power to see beyond the thin veil of the earth plane."

The inquisitive Irene Hughes wanted to know who Kaygee had been while on the earth plane. The spirit teacher gave her the name and address of his daughter, who, at that time, was in the United States, studying at Cornell University.

"Write to her," he bade Irene, "and she shall verify who I was on the earth plane."

In five days, Irene received a reply from the girl, verifying that she was indeed Kaygee's daughter. She said that her father had been one of the greatest Japanese Christians who had ever lived and that he had died in April of that year, 1961.

"The fact that the name and address of the daughter were correct seemed to me to be most evidential of Kaygee's survival after death," Irene said. "I had to accept the fact that his spirit was coming to work through me. He had lived a life of poverty and he had given his life to help others.

Perhaps he felt that I was so physically, emotionally, and psychically constructed that he could work through me. I considered myself honored that he had chosen me as a channel by which he might continue certain facets of his work."

"In life," Kaygee once told Irene, "I fought for the living truth in slums and along the highways. I met with opposition, but now I am at peace, for I know that my work will go on, through you and others like you. You, Irene, are a prophet, so filled with the knowledge of love and life that you are my vibratory equal. I have chosen you to work through."

Although Irene often goes into light trance, she does not seem to employ Kaygee in the manner in which the majority of mediums utilize their spirit guides. Usually, when a medium has entered trance, the personality of the spirit guide will assume control of the seance and temporarily possess the medium's body. The voice generally will no longer be that of the medium's, but will be altered to some degree indicative of another personality. It seems that Kaygee is "teacher," rather than "guide," and he seldom manifests to control the voice, facial features, or mannerisms of Irene Hughes. We have been present at only one seance when Kaygee came through and that was only for a brief time and to deal specifically with a matter that was of great importance to one of the sitters.

Over a friendship that has endured many years, we have asked Irene Hughes such questions about mediumship as the following:

From what source do you consider your abilities to be derived?

Irene Hughes: The gift of intuition is one of God's original gifts to all humankind. I have had mystical communication with a Divine Intelligence, whom I call God; and I also gain many of my talents through telepathic communication and through assistance from spirit intelligences. You know, of course, about Kaygee, my Japanese spirit guide and teacher.

Do you feel that your mediumistic or psychic gifts are compatible with organized religion?

Irene: Oh, I definitely feel that they are, but I also feel that these gifts transcend certain organized beliefs.

Do you honestly believe that there is a part of us that survives physical death?

Irene: Yes, it is the soul or spirit—that which is within us, unseen, but felt.

What is your understanding of "heaven," the afterlife?

Irene: I certainly do not visualize any geographical location. What is commonly called "heaven" is, I believe, a state of consciousness both here and after physical death. The afterlife is another experience in the evolution and growth of the Soul as it reaches toward Christlike perfection.

How do you perceive yourself as a medium?

Irene: I believe that I am basically honest and extremely loyal to my beliefs and my friends. I feel that I have a sincere spiritual love for all human beings. I respect all people because of my belief that the Christ Consciousness is within each of us.

I believe that each being is guided from within in moments of crisis. I would always act according to the guidance which was given to me at that crisis moment. I believe that such guidance would come from the original survival abilities instilled through, or within, the faculties of perception, which come from acknowledging God.

IS THERE A MEDIUMISTIC DOORWAY BETWEEN DIMENSIONS?

The one fact connected with all mediumistic phenomena, which both psychical researchers and spiritists will admit, is that there is an intelligence which directs and controls them. Another point of agreement is that this intelligence is a human intelligence characterized by the limitations, imperfections, and psychological drives of *homo sapiens.* The area of dispute lies in whether that human intelligence issues from the living or from the dead.

One point that has always struck us as interesting is that spirit communication through a medium still requires both a soul and a body— the soul of the alleged discarnate entity and the body of the medium. In the normal, living human, of course, the two are united and work together in harmony. But if we accept the spiritistic hypothesis, the production of phenomena, especially that of a physical nature, still requires the utilization of the medium's body and subconscious.

When one looks at the enigma of mediumistic phenomena from this point of view, one is able to understand quite fully the opinion of certain researchers who state that if a temporary union of discarnate entity and human body are necessary to produce spirit contact, then any sensitive human being should be able to manifest the same kind of phenomena. Each sensitive human has by his or her very nature a combination of soul and body. As we have seen throughout this book, the soul of the deceased, in temporary contact with a sensitive loved one's body, has the power to produce mediumistic phenomena and allow communication with the undying love energy of the dead.

When examining the enigma of mediumistic phenomena, we find ourselves continually confronted by great questions: Are mediumistic phenomena representative of humankind's own powers of transcendent mind, *i.e.*, telepathy, clairvoyance, precognition? Or do these manifestations provide the tangible evidence of the direct interaction of a human's physical body and the discarnate spirit of a deceased personality?

Modern humanity seeks the answer to the mystery of life beyond the grave as earnestly as did his ancestors. The will to believe is strong. Those men and women whose stories we have reported in this book have been blessed with their own personal and powerful proofs of the survival of their loved ones beyond physical death. It may well be that certain gifted mediums have been granted spiritual keys that permit them easier access to those mystical doorways between dimensions.

36

Ministering Angels
and Deathbed Comforters

A very old spiritual tradition says that at the time
of our birth each of us receives a guardian angel
who stays with us throughout our lives and who
ushers us to the Other Side at the time of our
physical death. Psalms 91:11 tells us that God
shall "give his angels charge" over us, to keep us
safe in all our ways.

So many people who have shared their moving
stories of undying love have told us of seeing
an angel or spirit guide interacting with their
loved one at the time of his or her graduation to
the higher dimensions. Although there are some
who believe that the interaction of angels and
humankind was limited to biblical times, we take
issue with that viewpoint. In our opinion, angelic-
spiritual interaction and intercedence has never

ceased—and as a matter of fact, has dramatically increased in recent years.

AN ANGEL CALLED HER SON'S SPIRIT FROM HIS BODY

Loretta Simms of Dayton, Ohio, saw an angel in the sickroom of her son twelve hours before his death. It was the angel, she testified, who called him out of his body.

Mrs. Simms stated that she too, lost consciousness and was taken out of her body by the angel. For several hours she was with her son in the spirit world. Here, she said, she saw many angels and spirit beings, who finally told her that she must return to her body. She bade her son farewell, and she was soon in her flesh form once again.

SHE SAW MOMMY AND SISTER TAKEN INTO THE SKY

Richard Riggs' wife and nine-year-old daughter were killed in an automobile accident and his six-year-old girl was severely injured. Riggs entered little Robin's hospital room and steeled himself for the awful task of informing her about the death of her mother and sister.

But before he could break the sad news to Robin, she told him that she already knew about the deaths. "While I was on the ground, Daddy," she began, "I saw an angel come to get Mommy. The angel started to go back up into the sky, but then it stopped, came back for Becky, and took both of them into Heaven."

"I WON'T NEED TOYS IN HEAVEN"

Pastor Burt Raymond had known for several months that his child, David, would not recover from his lengthy illness.

One warm July night, the family decided to sleep all in one room which was somewhat cooler than the others. Pastor Raymond said that he and his wife were both awakened by a soft tapping at the window near their bed. They then saw an angel come through the window, walk over to the sleeping boy, kiss him, and leave.

A few days later, in an effort to divert his mind from his illness, a friend asked David what he wanted for Christmas. The boy shook his head soberly and replied: "I'll be in Heaven. I won't need any toys there."

Within a week, David Raymond died.

A MYSTERIOUS KNOCK AT THE DOOR

Mrs. Dwight Morris of Lincoln, Nebraska, said that her daughter was caring for the younger child of neighbor in a nearby park when a blue-eyed, golden-haired angel appeared beside them. The angel knelt and kissed the child.

That night, according to the child's parents, a knocking was heard at their front door. When they answered the knock, they found no one there. In a few minutes, the sound was heard again.

On an impulse, the mother went into the room where her daughter was sleeping. To her great sorrow, she found that the child was dead.

Later, the two families reasoned that they had heard the angel knocking as it came for the spirit of the child, then rapping again as it left.

"DON'T WORRY—THE ANGELS HAVE SENT FOR ME"

Cleo Dewitt told of a dream that provided her with the information that her sister Beatrice was dying. Since she had experienced similar dreams before the deaths of other members of her family, she was inclined to pay heed to the nocturnal revelation. When a telegram arrived which confirmed Beatrice's approaching death, Cleo and her husband Martin left immediately to be at her sister's bedside.

Beatrice's eyes did not open, but she seemed somehow to know who was present in her room and even to know where they were standing. As Cleo bent to kiss her cheek, Beatrice spoke in a voice barely audible: "Don't worry, sis, they have sent for me."

Martin was standing by the window when Beatrice asked him to step aside so the angel might enter to take her home.

Confused, Martin moved back from the window, and all those present in the room were startled when a whiff of sudden wind stirred the curtains at the same time that the breath of life left Beatrice's body.

"My sister's face bore a lovely and restful smile as her soul left with her angel guide," Cleo Dewitt said.

THE RESEARCH OF
REV. W. BENNETT PALMER

Some years ago, Rev. W. Bennett Palmer, a retired Methodist minister, told us that his lifelong research into the appearance of angels and deathbed visions, had led him to record that the person who is about to transcend the physical shell often mentions a final boundary. After the dying person has passed that line of demarcation, he cannot return to the physical body. In fact, he is sometimes turned back before he can reach it again.

The environment and the scenery described in deathbed visions and in trance visions may be said to be much like the scenery of Earth—only it becomes more beautiful as the spirit progresses. Eventually, the environment becomes ineffable, incapable of description in human terms or in earthly comprehension.

In instances wherein it appears that one has achieved a glimpse into Heaven, the forms of loved ones and esteemed or saintly figures are often seen. Angels are very often described in the company of deceased loved ones. The angels may come to sing heavenly music, to summon the soul from the dying body, or to accompany the newly released spirit to the other world. Most of the men and women who have perceived the angelic death-bed comforters are able to describe the beings in great detail, including their eyes, hair, wearing apparel, and other attributes and accouterments.

ANGELS AT HIS DYING WIFE'S BEDSIDE

Max Gunderson told of the following visitation at his wife's deathbed:

"I saw three separate clouds float through the doorway into the room where my wife lay dying. The clouds enveloped the bed.

"As I gazed through the mist, I saw a woman's form take shape. It was transparent and had a golden sheen. It was a figure so glorious in appearance that no words can describe it.

"The beautiful entity was dressed in a long, Grecian robe, and there was a brilliant tiara on her head. The angel remained motionless with its hands uplifted over the form of my wife, seemingly engaged in prayer. Then I noticed two other beautiful angels kneeling by my wife's bedside.

"In a few moments there appeared above the form of my wife a spirit duplicate lying horizontally above it. It seemed to be connected to her body by a cord.

"The whole experience lasted for five hours. As soon as my dear wife had taken her last breath, the three angels and the spirit form of my wife vanished."

"I HAVE COME TO TAKE YOU HOME"

Reverend G. Maurice Elliott and Irene H. Elliott state that they were present at the bedside of a dying woman when an "angel-visitant" appeared to stand near her and say, "I have come to take you home."

According to the minister and his wife, three other angels and the images of many deceased friends and relatives of the dying woman were then seen to join the angel-visitant. A white, hazy mist rose above the woman, hovered there for a few moments, and eventually congealed to take on perfect human form.

After the soul-body had been released from its physical shell, the woman's spirit left in the company of the angels and those dear ones who had already become citizens of a higher dimension.

THE ANGEL RETURNED FOR HER BABY BROTHER

Edna Carney said that when she was eleven-years old her parents adopted Michael, a baby boy whom all the family loved very much. Edna remembered, however, that the baby's skin had a waxen pallor that worried her mother and their family doctor.

For a time the baby seemed to improve. Then one night, Edna and her mother were about to retire when they heard a firm knock on the door. They had been facing the door, so they were startled when they heard the latch click and they saw the door slowly swing open.

An angelic figure in shining white robes entered the room and closed the door slowly behind it. Without a word, the light being crossed the room and went over to where the baby lay sleeping. The angel reached out as if to take the baby, then lowered its arms and turned to walk away.

Halfway to the door, the angel turned to face the wide-eyed mother and daughter, then it disappeared.

Edna recalled that she was so frightened that her teeth were chattering. At last her mother broke the silence by questioning Edna whether or not the experience had been real and whether or not it had been shared. Edna replied that she had, indeed, seen the angel, and she expressed her opinion that the being had wanted the baby.

At that moment, the baby began to moan and to toss restlessly in its crib. For three days, two doctors sought to save little Michael's life. Then, on a Sunday evening, the baby boy smiled . . . and died.

For twenty years, Edna has remained convinced that the being did return for her little brother. In her interpretation of the incident, the angelic entity's initial visit was intended to prepare the family for the tragic event that was soon to come. Edna also testified that the experience had deepened her family's faith in the higher world.

AN ANGEL'S SONG
OF HEAVENLY PROMISE

Pastor Tom Vickdahl shared an account from Depression days when a poor family in Oklahoma suffered the additional hardship of losing a young daughter to typhoid fever. The family so desperately wanted a good Christian burial service for their Suzanne, but clergymen were almost nonexistent in that area during those troubled financial times.

A friend with an old Ford, barely held together with baling wire, volunteered to drive to a nearby village and do his best to convince some member of the cloth to accompany him back to a deserted church where the mourners would be waiting.

The sun was moving low on the horizon, and neither the friend nor the preacher were in sight. The mother was broken-hearted, and the few assembled mourners were becoming despondent.

Then a beautiful woman appeared outside the old church. No one saw where she came from and no one knew who she was. She walked inside the church, stood before the casket, and sang a lovely hymn, rich with spiritual meaning and comfort.

When she had completed the hymn, she walked away and seemingly disappeared. No one in that region ever saw her again. The impression that remained firm in the minds of the witnesses was that they had heard a song of heavenly promise from a ministering angel.

A BEAUTIFUL LADY IN WHITE CAME TO TAKE THE CHILD

Dr. Marshall Oliver told of the time that he was visiting a sick child, who had been slowly dying of complications suffered from pneumonia. As he turned to pick up his medical bag, he saw a beautiful "lady" dressed in white approach the child's crib. Dr. Oliver knew that he was not observing any member of the family.

"The lovely being bent over the crib, took the spirit form of the child into its arms, then passed right through the wall with the child. When I recovered my mental equilibrium, I examined the child and found that it had died at that moment."

AN ANGEL SEVERED THE CORD BETWEEN THE PHYSICAL AND SPIRITUAL BODIES

Don Pendergraff said that directly above his dying brother Nick he saw a shadowy form floating in a horizontal position. The form became more definite until it became an exact counterpart of Nick's physical body.

"Then I clearly saw an angel materialize and sever a cord which appeared to connect Nick's spirit form with his physical body," Don stated. "Once the cord had been separated, Nick's spirit form and the angel disappeared together."

CROWNED WITH A FLORAL DIADEM

Dr. D. P. Kayser said that while attending the funeral of Dr. Costello, a colleague whom he had known for over thirty years, he perceived his friend's soul leaving the body.

"There was no question in my mind that Angelo was truly clinically dead before the funeral," Dr. Kayser stated, "but I had once heard it said that 'real death' is not accomplished until the soul actually leaves the body."

Dr. Kayser knew that his friend's life had been one of kindness and service. "Angelo had always been a sincere, practicing Catholic, but even so I was quite startled when I saw a group of white-robed children materialize with what seemed to be flowers woven of mingled sunbeams and roses. Assembled near the coffin were white-robed spirits whom I recognized as deceased friends and relatives of Dr. Costello's."

As the funeral service progressed, Dr. Kayser was somehow able to observe the process of death. "I saw a vapor or mist gradually rise from the body in the casket. When the transition had been completed, the mist gradually took on the image of Dr. Costello.

"Almost at that very moment, a very beautiful angel, robed in the purest white, approached the newly liberated spirit. In its hands, the angel bore a lovely wreath, the center of which supported a large white flower. With this floral diadem, the angel crowned the spirit body of Dr. Angelo Costello.

"When the spirit form was completely separated from the physical body, the image of my friend, together with the angels and the attending spirits appeared to float away."

37

Visions at the Time of Death

During the course of his extended research into reports of angelic visitations and deathbed visions, Rev. W. Bennett Palmer commented that in the typical account, a bedside witness sees a mist or a cloud-like vapor emerging from the mouth or head of the dying man or woman. The vaporous substance soon takes on a human form, which is generally a duplicate of the living person—only in many cases any present deformities or injuries are partially or wholly absent. Angels or spirits of deceased loved ones are often reported standing ready to accompany the newly freed spirit form to higher dimensions of light.

In numerous reports, the immediate process of death is not witnessed, but the deceased is seen leaving the earth plane for the higher world, most often accompanied by angelic beings. Frequently, such spirit and angel leave-taking is witnessed in the sky, but this seems to be a mode of disappearance, rather than an indication that Heaven is in any particular spatial area.

"The belief in the existence of a supernatural world lies back of all deathbed experiences," Rev. Palmer told us. "A fact often noted in connection with deathbed visions is that they are frequently quite different from a patient's delerium and are coherent, rational, and, on reflection, apparently real.

"It has also been observed that visions of the dying are different from visions of those who only think themselves to be dying," he continued. "Visions of the dying are similar to those who claim to have been out-of-the-body during altered states of consciousness.

"Revelations concerning the nature of the future life which are received in deathbed visions seem to be regarded with favor by all churches, and no stigma attaches itself to the deathbed visionary experience. Persons having deathbed visions often claim to have seen the dead—or what is so regarded—and to have had them reveal knowledge of events which could not be known in any normal way. Frequently, the person having a deathbed vision claims to see a person in spirit who is not known to be dead. Later, investigation proves that the person *was* dead.

"A class of visions closely related to deathbed visions is that kind of experience in which the living see those who have just died at the exact time of their physical deaths," Rev.

Palmer explained. "Accounts of this kind are innumerable and have been the subject of much study. There can be no question concerning the reality of this class of visions—most often termed 'crisis apparitions' or 'apparitions at the moment of death.'

"Another aspect of the deathbed visions," Rev. Palmer concluded, "involves visions of angels and other Holy Figures seen by other persons in the presence of the dying.

"The deathbed scene may also be seen by persons not in the presence of the dying ones, but at a distance. Persons at a distance may also go out of their bodies and be present in death rooms. They may not only see the dying, but also the spirits and angels who may be present in the room and which may or may not be visible to the dying person and to those at his bedside."

Bill Winstowne told Rev. Palmer that he saw the spirit of his brother as it was disengaging itself from the dying body. The cloud-like vapor took on human shape, clapped its hands for joy, then passed upward through the ceiling in the company of an angel.

Jerry Caldwell of Denver, Colorado, said that at the time of death of his ten-year-old son, he saw the child's spirit leaving the body as a luminous cloud and rise upward toward the ceiling.

In Rev. Palmer's church in New Port Richey, Florida, two members of the congregation, Mr. and Mrs. Symington, who were very ill, had been placed in separate rooms in their home to insure periods of peace and uninterrupted sleep for both of them.

One afternoon, as Mr. Symington lay back against the pillows of his bed, he saw the form of his wife pass through the wall of his room, wave her hand in farewell, and rise upward in the company of an angel.

In two or three minutes, the nurse came into his room and informed him that Mrs. Symington had passed away. "I know," he said, blinking back the tears. "She had had enough of this desperate struggle to maintain life. She came to say good-bye and to ask me to join her with the angels."

Mr. Symington died two days later.

When Mrs. Ernestine Tamayo entered the sick-room to bring her husband his newspaper, she saw a large, oval light emerging from his head. The illuminated oval floated toward the window, hovered a moment, then was met by a lovely angelic figure. Within seconds, both the oval of light and the angel had vanished.

"I knew that Miles was dead even before I reached my husband's bedside," she told Rev. Bennett. "I had seen his angel guide come to take him home."

A PREVIEW OF HEAVEN

Seventy-year-old Mrs. Millie Dorrance lay dying, and she felt her spirit leaving her body. As her consciousness seemed to bob somewhere between dimensions of reality, she saw a beautiful light descending toward her.

She was drawn toward the light, and as she came nearer, she perceived that the source of the illumination was the aura or radiance around an angelic being. Later, Millie would say that the angel was lovelier than any earth language could ever convey.

The angelic being carried a cross in one hand and a wand-like instrument in the other. The entity touched Millie with the wand, and she felt a warm vibration of holy love spread throughout her entire consciousness.

"The cross," the angel explained, "is the symbol of sacrificial love—without which there is no Heaven."

While she was out of her body, Millie Dorrance was taken by the angel to an ethereal abode.

"I saw a beautiful angel instructing children who had died so young that they knew little or nothing of the earthly life of Jesus," she said. "The instruction was given in what might be called spiritual moving pictures. The story of Jesus was presented very much like it is in the Bible, but it was depicted from a more heavenly point of view. I saw Jesus before his resurrection walking among the tombs and speaking of the dead which he had redeemed. I saw the picture-teachings of Jesus re-entering his body. I heard God's voice say, 'This is my beloved son, the hope of Israel, the bright morning star. Peace to the world.' "

Mrs. Dorrance was told that she must return to the earth to share her experiences with others.

She was extremely disappointed to learn that she was not yet ready for her graduation to the higher world, but she was given a golden goblet from which to drink a liquid which would provide her with the strength to endure the separation from Heaven and to perform her earth ministry.

Millie Dorrance was also given a definite time to stay on Earth—after which she was assured that she would return to Heaven. The angel who had been her guide in the ethereal world escorted her back to Earth, and Millie re-entered her body so that she might begin her true mission.

Mrs. Millie Dorrance served as an inspiration to all who knew her, and she never wavered in her account of her marvelous sojourn in Heaven.

Before she died for the *second* time at the age of eighty-four, Millie said, "I will praise my Heavenly Father, for my hope in Jesus is worth more to me than ten thousand worlds."

Then, being fully appraised of her allotted time, Millie Dorrance sang her favorite hymn and completed her final transition to the higher world.

38

Messages From Loved Ones Who Dwell on the Other Side

By means of the careful analysis of many hundreds of messages obtained from those men and women who have received spirit communications from their loved ones on the Other Side, it is possible to compile a kind of synthesis regarding certain aspects of life in the Next World. While the vast majority of messages are of an extremely personal, specific, and individual nature, there are a number of statements which have been corroborated from so many sources that it is difficult not to place a certain amount of credence in them.

"From what the spirit of my husband Sam has told me," Bridget Clements said, "Heaven seems to be the summation of perfect Harmony and Love. He says that it is a person's 'inner life' that makes for righteousness and happiness."

Ann Halvorson said that her mother's spirit informed her that the entities in Heaven were always busy with pleasant activities. "It seems as though the spirits in the Next World are always learning and continually engaged in meaningful pursuits and recreations."

"In Heaven," said Marion Palmer, "Love is the great guiding star. Love fills the spirit entities with the highest joy. The spirit of my sister Jackie has told me that the souls of all those in Heaven are filled with unimagined happiness. She said that the divine energy of living, being, and becoming permeate their essences with an intensity of which we on Earth can have no conception."

In a kind of spiritual consensus, Hell appears to be the negation of all virtues and pleasures. Rather than a specific place, it seems more to be a condition or state of being which embodies the summation of all misdirected energies, such as those of greed, lust, malice, hate, and jealousy.

At the moment of physical death, the spirits newly freed from the confines of flesh are profoundly influenced by the belief constructs which they maintained while on Earth. A good Roman Catholic, therefore, will often perceive a saint or the Virgin Mary waiting to welcome the new soul to the Next World. A practicing Jew may anticipate Moses or Father Abraham to appear to stretch forth a hand of greeting. A Protestant may perceive Jesus or an angel waiting to open the gates of Heaven. After the spirit has adjusted to existence in the afterlife, however, once vital matters of creeds and ecclesiasticisms seem to fade into matters of little or no importance.

According to numerous reports of spirit communication, a person does not go directly to Heaven after he dies. The newly deceased finds himself or herself in what is commonly referred to as "paradise."

"Georgia said that it is a kind of gathering place for all newly arrived spirits," Douglas Johnson said, referring to the communication that he had received from his wife in the Next World. "She said that the place has nothing to do with whether or not you lived a good life or a bad life. Everyone goes there, regardless. It is something like a kind of resting place before the spirit moves on."

Johnson stated that he had looked up the word "paradise" in a dictionary and discovered that it is a Persian word for a park or a garden.

"From what I can ascertain," he continued, "it is after the spirit entity has been deceased for a while that it begins to grow weary of the familiar scenes of life on earth. I am certain that it all depends upon the individual entity and the personal circumstances of his or her passing, but it seems that the spirits must be willing to set aside their material interests before they are ready to progress more completely into the Light of higher awareness."

Peggy Ann Lawrence said that she sometimes felt as though the communicating spirit of her husband Patrick found it impossible to convey the beauty and the brilliance of the next world in mere mortal words. "I am not certain if Patrick is simply unable to describe the wonder of the afterlife or if my finite mind is simply unable to grasp it all. Patrick told me that at first everything in the Next World was so marvelously different from existence on Earth that he found it impossible to grasp. Now, I fear that Patrick has given up the task of allowing me to perceive the glory of the afterlife. He said that I will just have to wait and see it all for myself."

An aspect of the afterlife that has been confirmed over and over again in spirit communications throughout history is that many entities, especially if they lived gross, material lives on earth, may remain unaware that they have passed over for many days, months, or even years.

Camille Armitage, who made her transition in September of 1987, told her sister Louise that many spirits remain oblivious to the death of their bodies because they may be in a kind of dreamlike state immediately upon their transition. According to Camille, "This kind of spirit dreaming is different from earth dreaming in that the dreamer will never again awaken to physical realities. When the spirit does awaken, it will do so in a world of new realities which are unknown to it. It will only be some time later that such materialistic entities will emerge from their stupor and gradually become convinced that they are no longer living in the physical world."

Another consensus derived from hundreds of alleged spirit messages is that the more spiritually attuned that people have lived their lives on earth, and the less their minds have been restricted to such material goals as the accumulation of wealth, the less they have sought the accomplishment of selfish aims, and the satisfaction of animal gratifications, the fewer will be their desires to return to the earth plane even for a visit. The more spiritually-minded the recently deceased entities, the more will their spirit essences be focused on the Next World and its noble aims.

As a general rule, the moment people die, regardless of the kind of life that they have led, a spirit entity, usually a friend or a relative, comes to meet the newly deceased and becomes a kind of guide, whose mission is to greet them, to comfort them, and to show them around. Without such guides, the recent arrivals would feel desperately lonely and confused the moment that they would wake up to their new life.

"My wife Ramona told me that she was met by her grandparents and by her best friend Carmen, who had been killed in a car accident two years ago," said Joaquin Sanchez. "I had been so sad, so frightened, until the spirit form of my wife told me that she was not alone on the other side. It brought me great peace, just knowing that she had someone with her."

Many of those who have received spirit communications have repeatedly assured their surviving loved ones that all the objects of the earth plane have their spiritual counterparts on the other side.

"We have our spirit form duplicates of everything that you can see around you," Edward

Balanzar heard the spirit voice of his wife Donna tell him. "We have trees, flowers, animals, mountains, rivers, and seas."

The inquisitive Balanzar insisted on hearing a more complete description of the environment of the next world.

"We have clouds and rainy days, storms and lightning," the spirit entity continued. "We have the thousand and one forms that make Mother Nature so beautiful. We have houses and books and clothes. Everything on Earth has its mental duplicate or counterparts in the spirit world."

In an interesting twist, Kathy Baxley said that her sister Barbara communicated from spirit that those of us who dwell on the physical plane are deemed "spooks" by the entities in the Next World. "Life is intensely pleasurable here," Barbara said from the other side. "Although you think of us over here as ghosts, to us it is the other way around. We look upon you as spooks and shadowy beings, because you are transparent to our mental vision. From our perspective, it is we who are the real thing. We appear to one another as perfectly solid."

The spirit being of Frank Manluccia appeared to his wife Teresa and told her that since spirits have no physical bodies, they have no nerves, and therefore cannot feel pain.

"Life cannot help being more virtuous here," he said. "Spirit entities do not harm or kill one another—because our bodies cannot be harmed or murdered. There is not the slightest temptation to steal, because there would be nothing to steal that we cannot form mentally with our own minds. It is pointless to tell lies, for the obvious reason that we can read one another's thoughts. We do not eat and drink, therefore drunkeness and gluttony cannot exist.

"Although we keep a concept of sexual identity, we do not marry. And because we have no physical bodies there can be no such things as adultery, lust, or jealousy. The concept of possesiveness of one another has completely disappeared. We are no longer attracted to the promise of the physical delights of the body, but to the prowess of one's mental strength and the beauty of one's soul."

Sherrana Park had been deceased for nearly three years before her spirit entity appeared to her husband Ronald. "Darling, if you can grasp the concept that thoughts are things, you will be in a marvelous position to understand many of the essential mysteries of the universe—including life after death," she told him. "Because of my more rapid ethereal vibration, I can appear before you in your more physically dense world. Likewise, I can easily walk through your doors and walls, because they are objects of the third dimension. I now exist beyond the fourth dimension."

"If you should encounter spirit entities who appear interested in matters of the flesh and who are selfish and exploitative," warned the spirit entity of Jack Kaska, "you have met beings from the lower and less spiritual planes of existence. On planes of higher spiritual vibration, love is the chief emotion."

"Like-minded souls are attracted to one another," Kris Caroselli's spirit essence communicated to her mother, Bernadette. "Here, the happiness of the soul depends upon its own resources. We do not work to earn money for the pleasures of existence. We are free to utilize our individual talents as we prefer. Because our thoughts and our characters are completely open and naked for all to see, there is no attempt at pretense. Spirits of similar vibrational frequencies just naturally move toward one another.

"Those souls who for whatever reason are slow to adjust to the Next World may stay on the lower planes for years. Some exist for quite some time in a kind of mental darkness. That is quite sad, for the heavenly life is one of growth in wisdom, insight, and love."

The spiritual essence of Floyd Arneson materialized to his wife Lillian to explain the three distinct realms or dimensions of spiritual expression.

"In the afterlife," he said, "there is the Etheric, the Mental, and the Spiritual. Your plane, my dear one, is the world of Matter, wherein you have a physical body that is controlled by your mind. On the other side, however, we manifest a mentally formed etheric body that is controlled by our spirituality. The key to all of this is to interpret the physical in terms of the mental—and control the whole by means of the spiritual."

*   *   *

According to Goldie Carneal, her father Aaron's spirit form told her that telepathy was the normal means of inter-communication among spirits and between spirit beings and humans.

"Telepathy dispenses with the clumsiness of language and renders sound superfluous," the entity said. "It is this mechanism that permits spirit entities to communicate with the living in whatever country they may exist. It is also such a mechanism that allows spirits from ancient times to be able to be understood by men and women in the twentieth century."

Al Munoz had been confined to a wheelchair for eleven years before he passed on in September of 1988. "Time and space do not have the same meaning over here," his spirit being told his wife Terry. "I can travel from one spot on the earth to another, simply by thinking it to be so. I'm not confined to that darn wheelchair any longer, darling, and I'm traveling all over the place now."

The spirit of Philip Anderson appeared to his wife Sonya and told her to go at once to her physician to have a lump in her left breast examined.

"Phil could see inside my body," Sonya said. "He explained that their sense of color is vastly superior to ours, and their range of sight extends far beyond our small share of the spectrum. Their sight moves beyond even what we know as the ultra-violet range. Phil said that everything that was around me in my environment appeared totally different to him—and different from the way that he had remembered it.

"Phil surprised me when he said that there was no sunlight in the Next World, but that everything was intensely bright, regardless. I guess that was why my physical body was more or less transparent to his spiritual eyes. His sight could penetrate between the molecules of my body, just like X-rays do."

Marie Remick's three children were all under five years of age when her husband Larry was killed in the Korean conflict in 1952. Even today, forty years later, Marie still feels the guiding and protecting influence and spiritual presence of her husband, and she feels that she knows why this is so.

"I have come to understand that when the spirits in the Next World develop spiritually, they pass to a higher spiritual sphere," Marie said. "Those spirits who graduate to that higher plane eventually lose all their interest in the mundane, the material, the earthly. The higher the spirits evolve, the less often they will be concerned with earth plane considerations. In fact, the highly progressed entities will rarely come to anyone on Earth *unless* there should be such a strong bond of affection between the spirit and those left behind that the entity will frequently return to monitor their loved ones—until the loved ones join them in the Next World. I know that Larry's spirit remains concerned about us and that he awaits our joining him on the other side."

Tiffany Tiers said that communication with the spirit essence of her husband Norman has emphasized to her that the principal difference between life on Earth and that of the other side lies in the fact that we exist in a physical world wherein everything is governed by physical laws.

"In the Next World," she stated, "the spirit beings live on a mental plane and thought replaces physical action and crude matter. Thoughts are things, and the limitations of time and space do not exist for them.

"Another main difference," she added, "is that over there, love is the principal energy that controls every thought, every deed, every vibration."

In his quest to solve the enigma of life after death, scientist George Lindsay Johnson thoughtfully observed what he believed to be an axiomatic truth: "The Universe is a vast exhibition of intense activity, movement, and intelligence—a *becoming* through perpetual evolution. This consists of two systems—the natural or physical, and the psychic or spiritual world—and each of them is governed by its own laws, which are entirely different in their action. These two world-systems are perpetually acting and reacting on each other; the physical world being subservient to the spiritual world, and controlled by it. Furthermore, the inhabitants of the spirit world are merely human beings freed from the limitations imposed upon them by their physical bodies."

* * *

Bishop Jeremy Taylor once said that love is the greatest thing that God can give us, for He himself is love. And love, he went on, is the greatest thing that we can give to God, for it will also give ourselves and carry with it all that is ours. Love is the old, the new, and the great commandment, and all the commandments, for it is the fulfilling of the law.

There does indeed appear to exist a great Divine Plan of Love that we cannot totally comprehend; but as we have seen throughout the pages of this book, some people have been blessed by receiving glimpses of this ultimate statement of immortality. Love can give us Heaven upon Earth, and the spiritual essence of certain men and women have so powerfully expressed their undying love that they have brought Heaven back to Earth and blended the two worlds into one.